Exotic Paper Airplanes

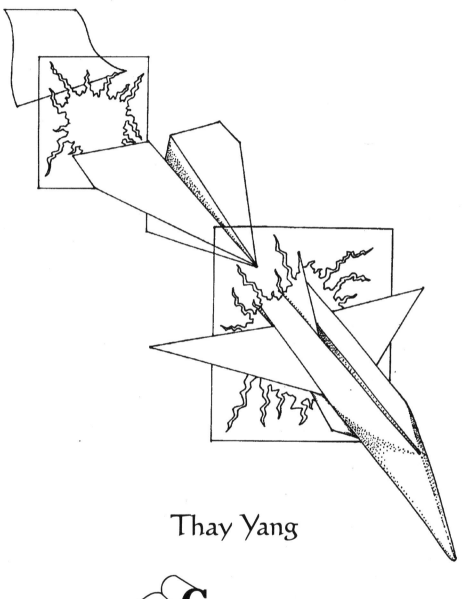

Thay Yang

Cypress House
Fort Bragg, California

Exotic Paper Airplanes

Copyright © 2000 by Thay Yang

Cypress House
155 Cypress Street
Fort Bragg, CA 95437

Printed in the United States of America

Library of Congress Cataloging-in-Publication Data

Yang, Thay.
    Exotic paper airplanes / Thay Yang -- 2nd ed.
     p.cm.
    ISBN 1-879384-346-1
     1.Paper airplanes. 2. Origami. I. Title.

 TL778.Y36 1999
  745.592 21--dc21   99-044734

Expanded Edition

Special Thanks to
Say Yang and Vun Yang

A Note from the Author

It gives me great pleasure to offer you these fifteen extraordinary aircraft for folding and flying. For some time I've dreamed of sharing the Asian art of paper folding, applied to both simple and sophisticated airplanes, as a way of demonstrating the magical uses of paper.

Paper that is neither written on nor read from can still educate and entertain. In the hands of a clever student, the folding and flying of *Exotic Paper Airplanes* can teach aeronautic principles while inspiring the imagination to soar.

Study the next few pages of terms, tips, and practice folds before starting your first plane. This will prepare you for the instructions to follow. Perfect the practice folds, then refer to them later if you experience difficulty with a plane. Once you have mastered the steps that are fully covered in the practice folds and the first two chapters (*Concord* and *Jet*), creating the rest of the planes should be easy.

I also urge you to fold the planes in sequence. You will need to become proficient with the simpler folding techniques of the first planes to conquer the more complex aircraft at the book's end.

After folding and flying these magnificent planes, you can experiment with various modifications. You may wish to change a plane's shape, combine different elements, or create entirely new airplanes. That's what I do. If you have patience and let your creativity fly, you too can push the envelope of paper flight.

Glossary

Aileron (or flap) = the hinged, movable trailing edge of a wing used to alter camber and, therefore, lift and drag, especially during landing.

Crease = the result of a fold.

Elevator = a horizontal control surface at the trailing edge of the plane that can be bent up or down to control or cause climbing or diving.

Fin = the upright part of the tail.

Fuselage = the body of the airplane.

Rudder = a vertical control surface at the trailing edge of the plane that can be moved to initiate a right or left turn.

Stabilizer = the fixed horizontal part at the tail of the plane.

Trim = fold or bend to control turning, climbing or diving.

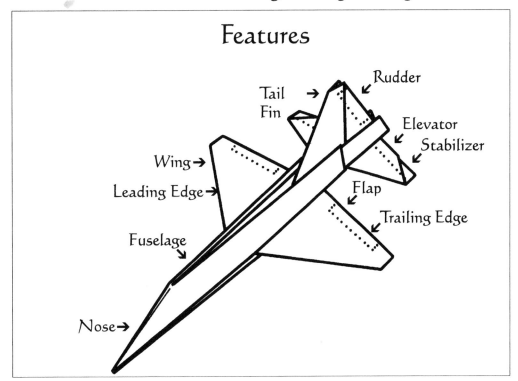

Features

Tail →
Fin
Rudder
Elevator
Stabilizer
Wing →
Leading Edge →
Flap
Trailing Edge
Fuselage
Nose →

Tips for Folding and Flying Paper Airplanes

1) Study the diagrams. Each one shows the result of the previous step and leads to the next. Looking ahead will help you see what the fold leads to. Follow the steps in order until the plane is finished.

2) Every fold should be made evenly and firmly. Use the back of your thunbnail to press the crease. To sharpen the crease line on a base fold or inside-reverse fold (to make the crease hinge backward easily later), run your fingernail over it several times.

3) Usually when making a fold on one side, you'll do the same to the other side, back to back. Making these "match-folds" exactly the same will produce an airplane that looks better—and flies better.

4) Making the fuselage is most important to finishing a plane. Work carefully, concentrating on the diagrams and following directions precisely. After you've mastered the inside-reverse and fuselage folds, the other folds will be easy.

5) Fold the tail fin straight up.

6) When flying, throw the plane straight out from your body.

7) Add weight (e.g., a paperclip) to the nose if the plane loops.

8) To make the plane climb when thrown, trim the elevators up. To make it dive, trim the elevators down.

9) For right or left turns trim the rudders to the right or left, respectively.

10) For stunts, trim one aileron down and the other up. This will make the plane spin and roll as it flies.

Indication of a
hidden fold

Fold line _ _ _ _ _ _ _ _ _ _ _ _ _ _ _

Crease line . . . .

Distance }

Inches = "

Fold direction ⟶

Fold back and forth
(or side to side) ⟵⟶

Fold behind

Fold then unfold ⟵▬▶

Turn model over

Unfold ⟶

Where to press your
thumb & index finger

Introduction

Beginning with the Wright brothers' first flight, airplanes have revolutionized the world. Aircraft of different types with very different purposes began appearing in and being tested by nations around the globe. The US F-14 Tomcat, the F-18 Hornet, Stealth fighters and other combat planes are high-performance descendants of our early aeronautic ancestors.

The industrialized nations of the world have a variety of defensive aircraft, including both fighters and bombers, with individualized style and appearance. All have made a significant impact on world power. Many youngsters dream about flying such aircraft, and if they are industrious and study hard they may someday realize their dream.

Right now, young and old alike can learn a great deal about aeronautics while enjoying the challenge of creating modern fighting aircraft through the secrets of paper airplane folding in this book. Never before have such compact and perfect paper airplanes been made.

In this expanded edition, you'll find clear diagrams and easy-to-follow instructions for folding replicas of the world's fastest and most powerful aircraft. Each plane is folded from a single sheet of paper without any cutting. No previous book offers the techniques for constructing paper aircraft that do not involve cutting (although optional cutting techniques are offered) or the use of more than one piece of paper. No other book offers such realism, in appearance as well as in flight. If you've ever wanted to learn how to fold *Exotic Paper Airplanes,* your fun-filled education is about to begin.

Practice Fold #1: Inside-Reverse Fold

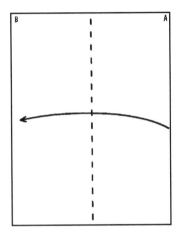

1) Fold the paper in half.

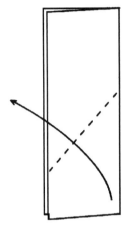

2) Fold the bottom half diagonally to the left side.

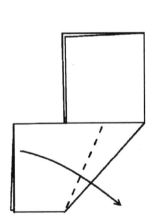

3) Fold diagonally back down.

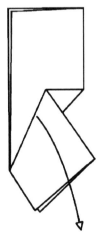

4) Unfold completely.

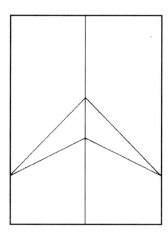

5) This is what the paper should look like with crease lines.

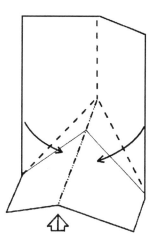

6) Fold the two sides together and raise up the center fold line.

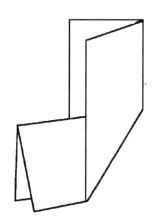

7) The fold looks like this.

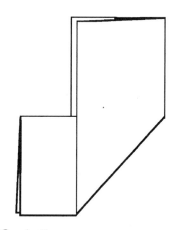

8) Push flat.

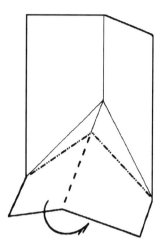

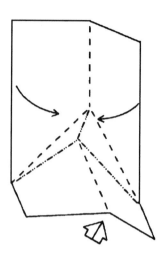

9) Open the paper halfway and fold inward on the marked crease lines.

10) Fold the two sides of the paper together again with the bottom part of the paper folding away to the back side.

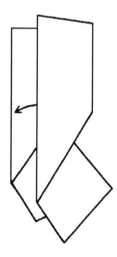

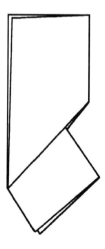

11) Close the paper tightly together.

12) Completion of inside-reverse fold. This is a vital folding technique, so try it a few times before moving on.

Practice Fold #2: The Fuselage Fold

The fuselage fold is vital— the essential element needed to fold the planes in this book. Two coordinates will be given, as in the wing fold. Practice the fuselage fold a few times before starting on any plane. After you've perfected this fold, you can easily fold any fuselage.

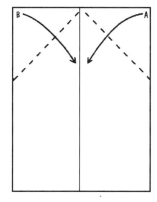

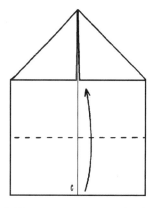

1) Begin with a center crease line. Fold corners A and B down to the center crease line.

2) Fold C up to meet with the horizontal bottom edge of A and B.

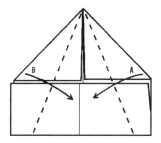

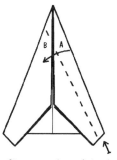

3) Fold A and B to the center line.

4) The coordinates for this fold are 2" down from the tip and ½" at the pivot point (indicated by the small arrow). Fold side A.

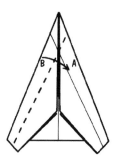

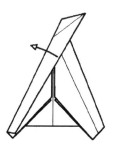

5) Unfold.

6) Fold side B.

7) Unfold.

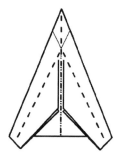

8) This diagram shows the two resulting crease lines crossing.

9) Make an inside-reverse fold using the existing creases. The mountain crease rises up between the two outside edges. (Note: this is the fuselage reverse fold. The fuselage folds for the planes in this book have similar diagrams but different coordinates.)

10) Proceed through the fold.

11) Flatten loosely.

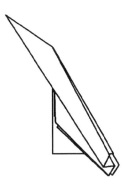

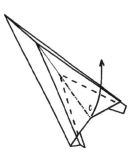

12) Fuselage fold completed.

13) The tail fin of the plane. Here the inside-reverse fold is going up.

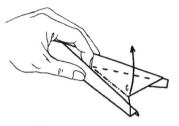

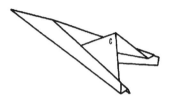

14) To make this reversal, hold the nose end of the plane with your left hand. Place your index finger in the center crease line as shown here. Hold the plane tightly at the nose end, and control the size of the tail fin by sliding your index finger up or down the center crease line. At the lowest point of the belly, reverse it straight up the center with your right hand.

15) The inside-reverse fold looks like this.

16) Completed tail fin fold.

Practice these last few important folds a few times until you are confident. Now you're ready to start folding real planes. You've earned your wings!

Contents

CONCORD

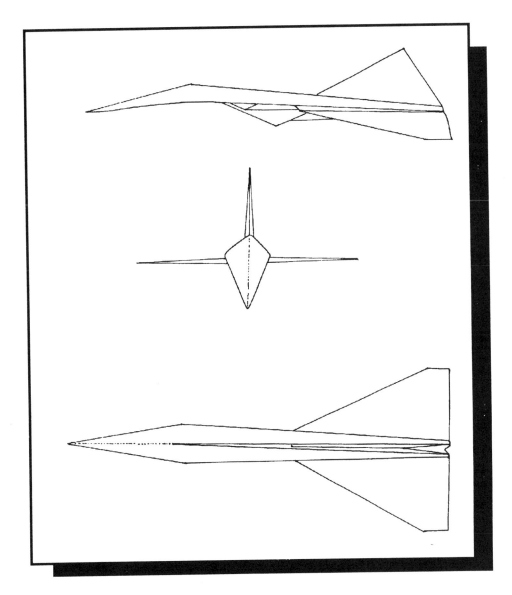

This plane is the simplest to fold of all the planes in this book. It uses basic folding techniques employed throughout the rest of the book. To be successful, follow the steps carefully and precisely. The most important element is to pull up the nose of the plane, and carefully press and align the back, as shown in the drawings. Also, make sure both sides are folded evenly on every fold throughout the plane assembly. Mastering the steps displayed in drawings 16 through 22 in the Concord will greatly improve your future foldings.

NOTE: I suggest that you fold this plane at least five times before going on to other planes.

1) Lay an ordinary piece of
8 1/2 x 11 paper on a flat surface.

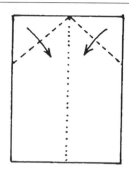

4) Now, unfold the paper and fold down
the top corners as indicated by the arrows.

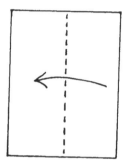

2) Fold the paper in half.

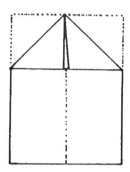

5) Your fold should look like this.

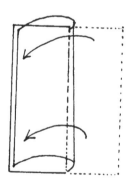

3) Your fold should look like this.
Make sure it's folding evenly.

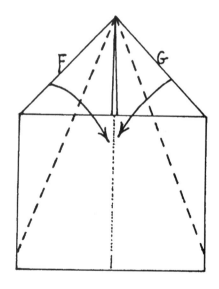

6) Fold the two edges, F & G,
toward the center line, as indicated.

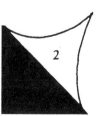

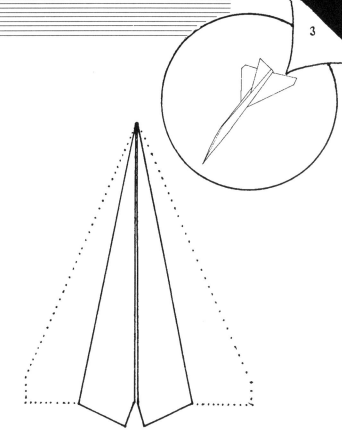

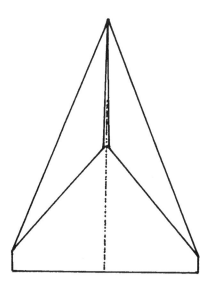

7) It should now look like this.

9) After folding toward the center line, the paper should look like this.

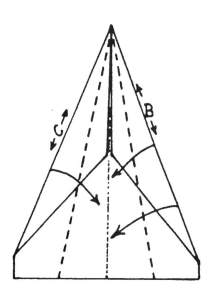

8) Now, fold the two sides, B & C, in toward the center line.

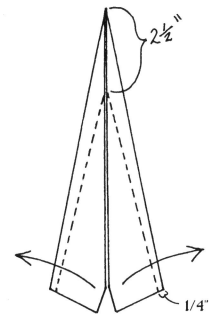

$2\frac{1}{2}"$

$1/4"$

10) Fold the wings out 2 1/2" from the tip as shown by the two big arrows.

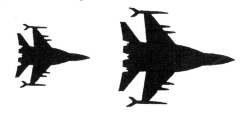

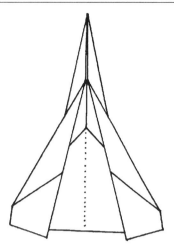

11) Your folded wings should look like this.

14) After you have folded the nose down, fold the two sides of the plane toward the back as indicated, along the center line.

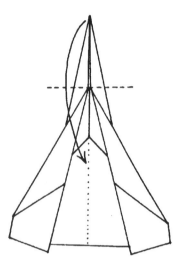

12) About 2" from the top, fold down on the dotted line.

15) It should look like this from the side. Pull up the nose as shown by the arrows.

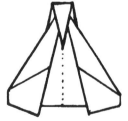

13) Your fold should look like this. Once you've mastered folding the Concord, make just a 90 degree fold here.

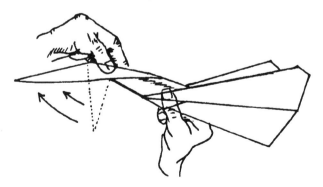

16) Pull up the nose like this.

4

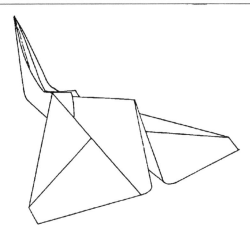

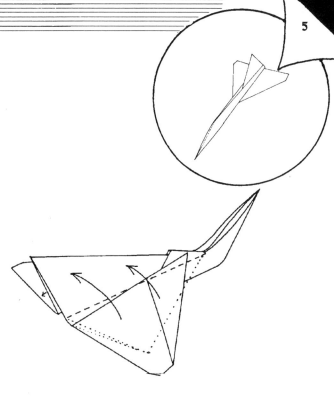

17) Now, place the plane upside down on a flat surface.

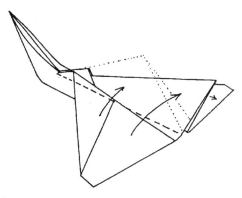

18) Place both of your hands exactly as shown here and hold the plane tightly. Fold back and forth on the dotted line three times on each side.

20) Fold it to the left as shown, then to the right. This sets the back into position. Note: Steps 17 to 20 here should be used for All planes in this book.

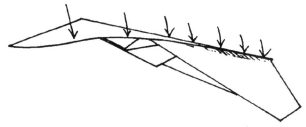

21) Now, flip the plane upright again and press the back down and together as indicated by the arrows.

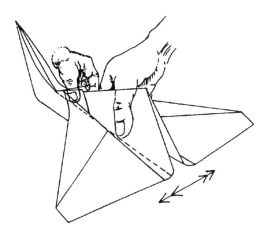

19) Fold it to the right as shown here, and then to the left.

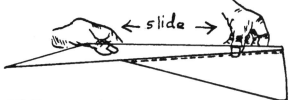

22) Now, carefully line up the back of the plane by sliding your left hand back and forth as shown here. Then fold the wings up on the dotted line.

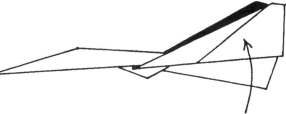

23) Your folded wings
should look like this.

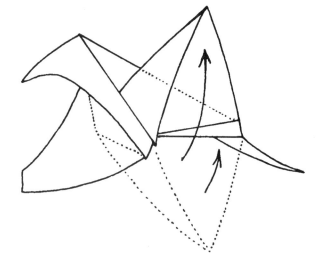

26) Now, carefully lift the tail
(fin upward) on the dotted line
as indicated here from the rear view.
Note: Once you know how to pull up
the tail fin, you won't need
to fold it back and forth first.

24) To make a tail fin, fold the tail back and
forth three or four times at the dotted line.

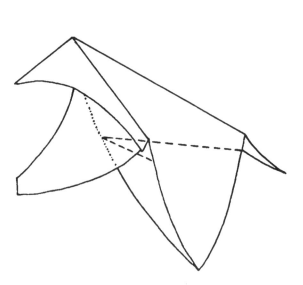

25) After folding the tail
back and forth a few times,
it should look like this from the rear.

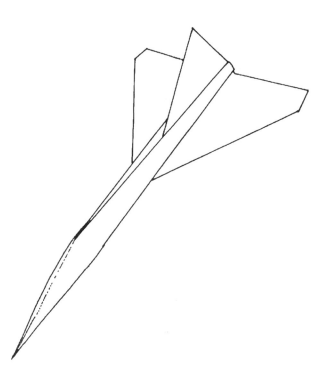

27) Finished version!

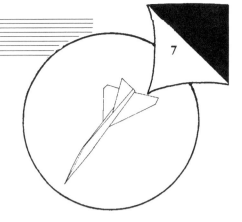

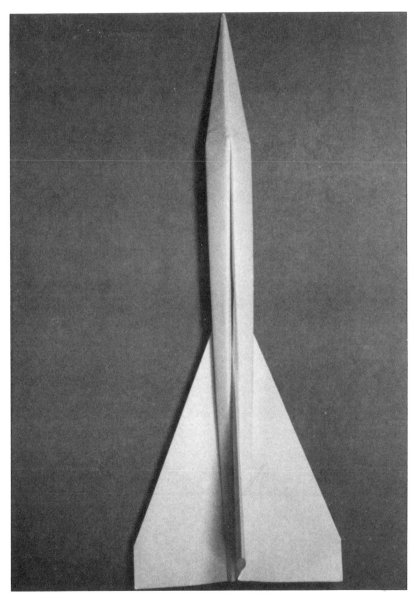

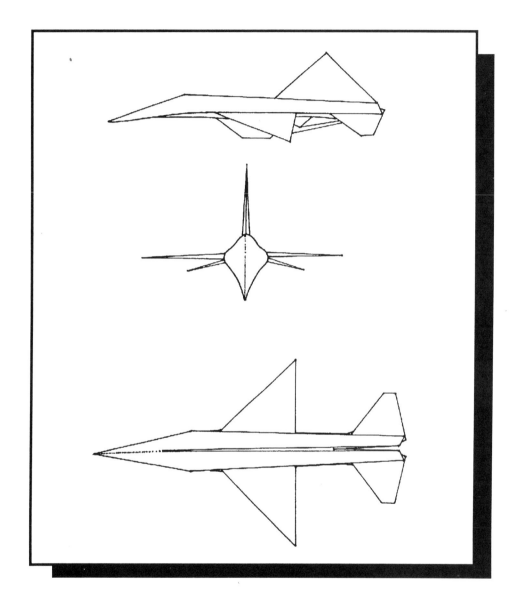

The Jet is the second primary plane that you must know how to fold before going on to other planes. Carefully follow all the steps and diagrams. Remember, always make sure that all folds are even. Use the techniques you learned from the Concord to help you align the back. (NOTE: occasionally, you will need to repeat the steps from the Jet section on the planes ahead.)

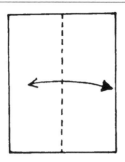

1) Fold paper in half, then unfold.

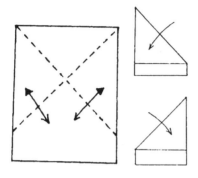

2) Fold diagonally at dotted lines, then unfold.

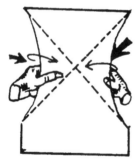

3) Now, use both hands and fold the paper up and in toward the middle.

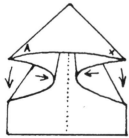

12) This is how the paper should look. Gently press down from the top.

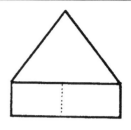

5) Now, it should look like this.

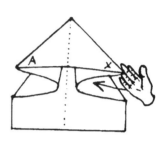

6) Slide your right hand under Flap X as shown here.

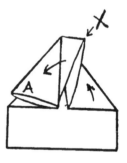

7) Flip Flap X over and onto Flap A.

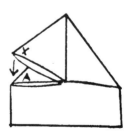

8) Flap X should line up evenly with Flap A on the left side.

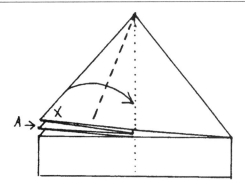

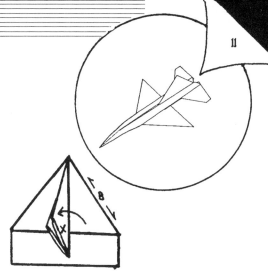

9) Now, fold Flap X on the dotted Line toward the center Line.

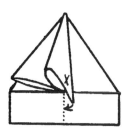

10) This is how your fold should look.

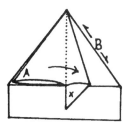

11) After you have folded Flap X toward the middle flap, flip it to the right side. Notice the B Edge.

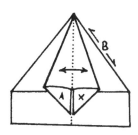

12) Now, repeat Steps 9-11 for the left side, and open the flaps to look like this.

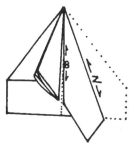

13) Now, flip Flap X to the left, over Flap A again.

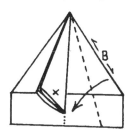

14) Then fold side B on the dotted Line to the center Line.

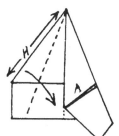

15) Now it should look like this.

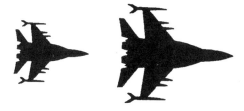

16) Now, flip both Flaps A & X to the right side. Repeat Step 14 for the left side.

17) Spread Flaps A & X apart like this.

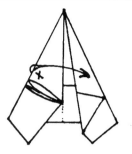

20) Now, flip Flaps A & X to the right.

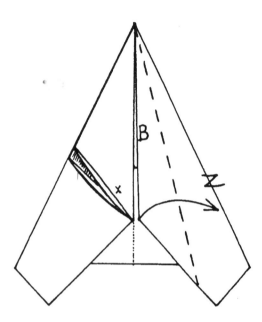

18) Now, flip Flap X to the left side.
Then fold Edge B on the dotted Line
and match it evenly with Edge Z.

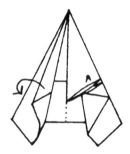

21) Repeat Step 18 on the left side.

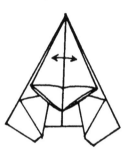

22) Then spread the flaps as shown here.

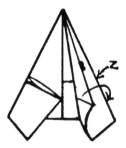

19) This is how the fold should look.

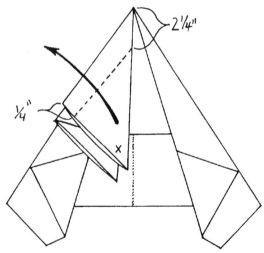

23) Now, you're going to carefully fold
the wings out. Fold Flap X to
the left side on the dotted Line.

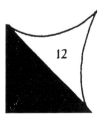

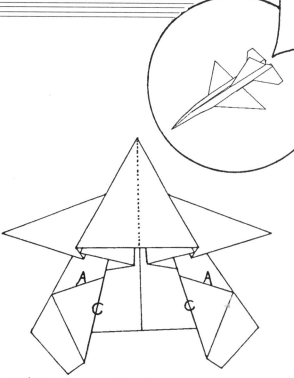

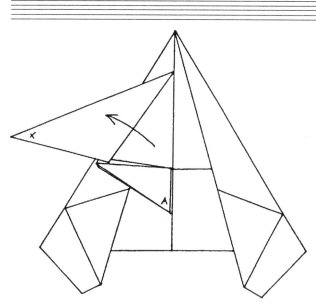

24) Your folded wing should look like this.

25) Now, flip Flap X to the right side.

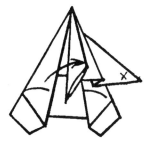

26) Also flip Flap A to the right.
Fold Flap A so it matches up evenly
with Flap X on the right side.

27) Now, move Flap A back to the left
so it looks like this. Label A's and C's
if you wish.

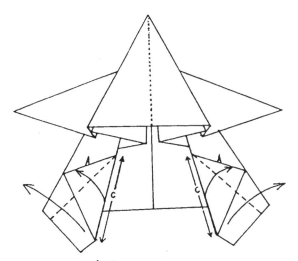

28) Now you're going
to fold the stabilizers.
Fold Edge C evenly toward Line A.

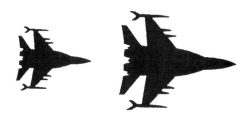

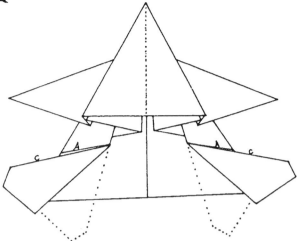

29) Make sure your folds are even.

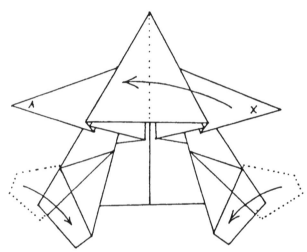

30) Now, unfold the stabilizers and flip Wing X to the left side.

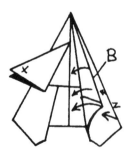

31) Flip Edge B to the middle.

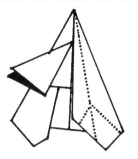

32) You should have three crease lines as shown here.

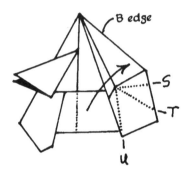

33) Unfold the B edge further and you should see the crease lines – S, T & U.

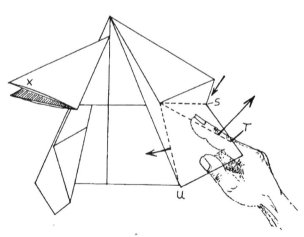

34) Put your index finger on the middle of Line T and push it outward while pushing Lines S & U inward as indicated by the arrows.

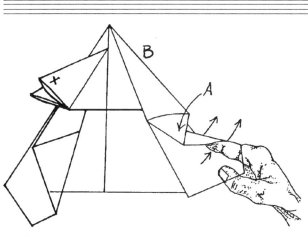

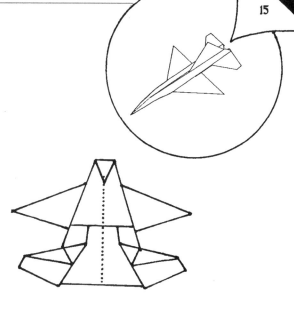

35) Your plane should look like this after you push out Line T. Press down on Point A. Repeat Steps 32-36 on the left side.

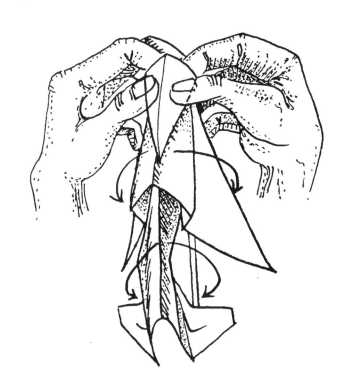

38) Your fold should look like this.

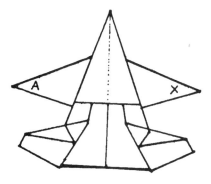

36) Open Side A to the left side so the plane looks like this.

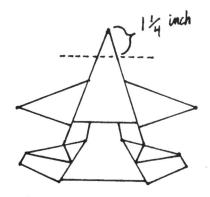

37) Measure about 1 1/4 inches from the end of the nose. Fold down the nose along the dotted line.

39) After folding down the nose, fold both sides of the plane's body toward the back as shown.

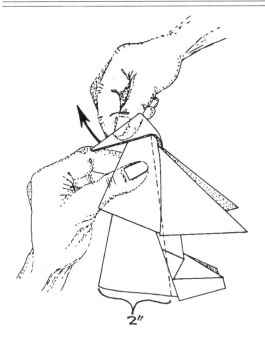

2"

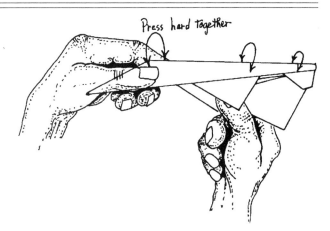

Press hard together

42) Move your right hand under the wings.

40) From the side, your plane should look like this. Now, hold the body with your left hand, and, with the other, pull up the nose. Then, as you did on the Concord (Steps 17-20), lay the plane, upside down, on a flat surface and fold the under fuselage back and forth. (This method is used on all the planes in this book.) Notice the 2-inch depth.

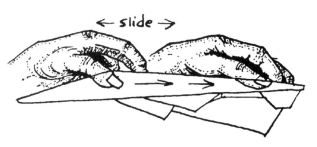

← slide →

43) Carefully apply pressure while sliding your left hand along the back of the plane.

41) Continue to grip the plane firmly in your left hand while using the thumb and index finger of your right hand to press hard along the plane's body, as shown here.

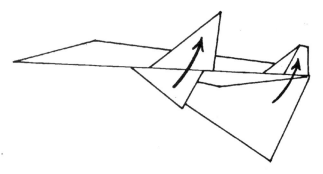

44) After you have completed the back, fold up the wings in the front and back as shown.

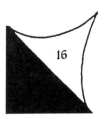

16

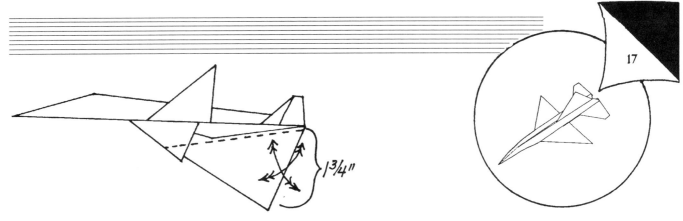

$1^{3/4}"$

45) Fold along the dotted line four times from side to side.

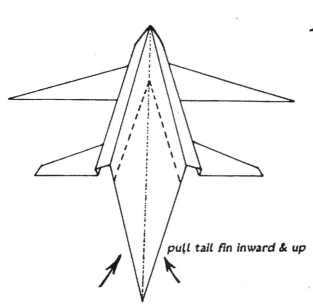

pull tail fin inward & up

46) This is the rear view of the plane. Lift the tail inward & up as indicated by the arrows.

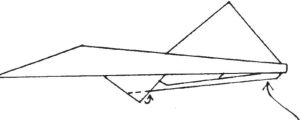

48) Fold the belly inward 1/2 inch, along the dotted line. You can tape here to bond the two sides together. Taping improves flight performance. You can tape all other planes, except the Hornet, in the same place.

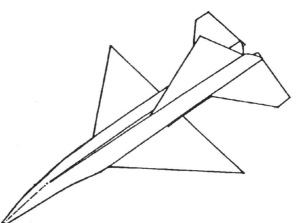

49) The finished version of the Jet. Turn to page 85 and round the nose as shown for the Hornet on Step 35.

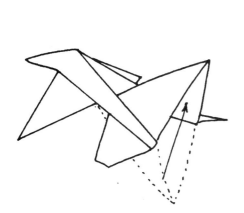

47) Your tail fin should come up like this.

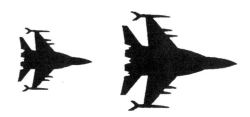

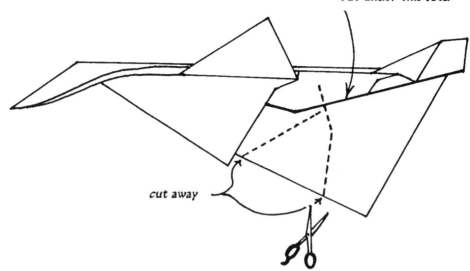

cut under this fold

cut away

50) You are now finished with the Jet, a highly original plane. If you want the tail to look more realistic, pull it down the way it was before you raised it, then cut along the dotted lines and push it up again. Make sure that it's even with the body. (NOTE: this tail-cut technique may also be used on the Mig-27.)

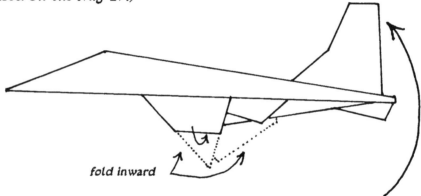

fold inward

51) Bring the tail up like this.

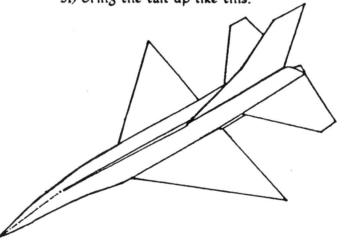

52) The new tail of the Jet.

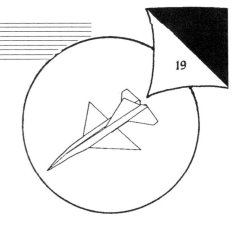

SHUTTLE

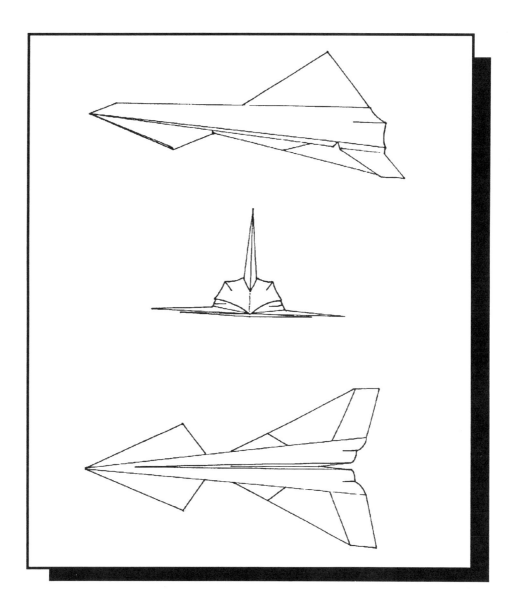

In making the Shuttle, the first few folds are exactly the same as the Jet's,
so turn back to the Jet and follow Steps 1-22. Then come back here and continue.

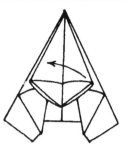

1) This is how your paper should look after completing Steps 1-22 in the Jet chapter. Now fold Flap X to the left as the arrow indeicates.

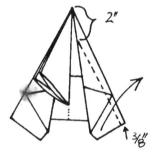

2) Fold the right wing out to the right along the dotted line.

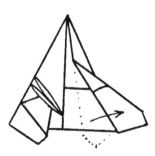

3) Your right wing fold should look like this. Now make the same fold on the left side.

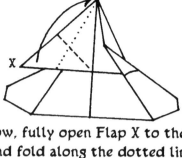

4) Now, fully open Flap X to the left and fold along the dotted line so that Corner X is on Corner H.

5) This is how your fold should look. Do the same on the other side.

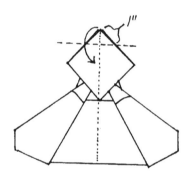

6) Separate your newly folded flaps. This is the front stabilizer. Fold the nose along the dotted line.

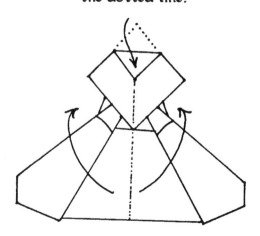

7) This is how the fold should look. Now fold both sides of the plane away from you.

22

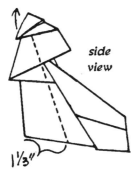

side view

1 1/3"

8) The plane should look like this. Next, turn the plane over and pinch the belly about 1 1/3" into the fuselage (along the dotted line) while you press the back of the plane against your work surface.* Fold the belly from side to side a few times. As you did with the Jet, pull up the nose and pinch the fuselage together. *(Note: this will properly align the tail and the wings.

11) Make another fold as shown here for the engine.

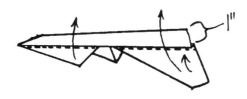

1"

9) After you have pulled up the nose, line it up with the back. Then fold the wings up. You can now push the tail fin up.

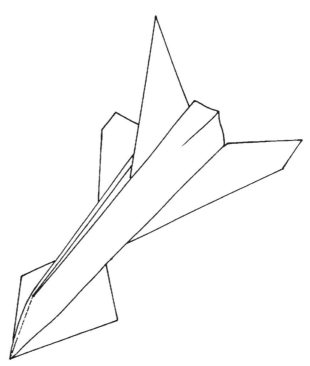

12) The finished version of the Shuttle.

10) With the tail pulled up, the plane should look like this.

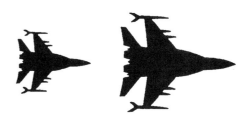

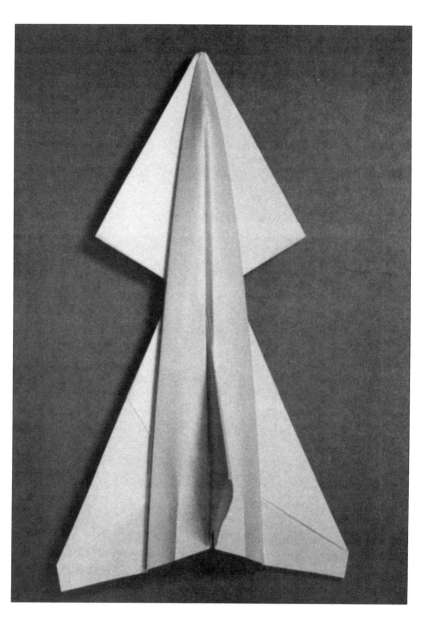

13) This airplane will fly as well as the real Shuttle!

FUTURE FIGHTER

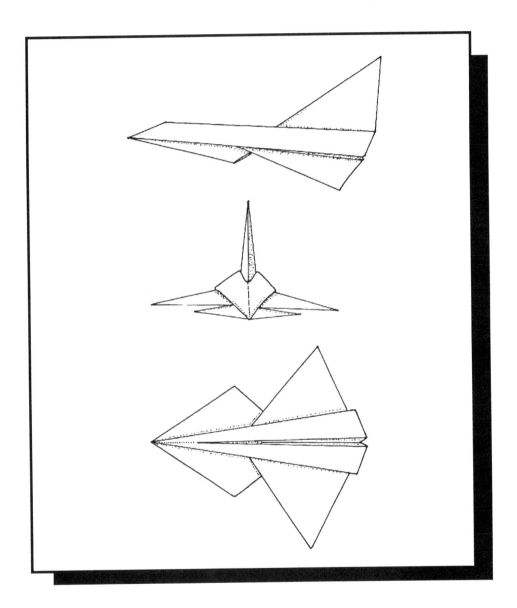

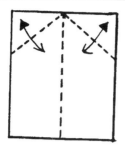

1) Fold the paper in half. Unfold it, then fold down the two corners.

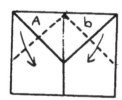

2) Fold down on the dotted line.

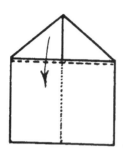

3) Fold the corners diagonally again.

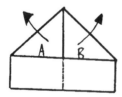

4) Your fold should look like this. Now, unfold the corners again.

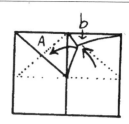

5) Put your hand under the Side B fold, then lift and reverse the fold to the left, as shown.

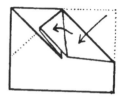

6) The fold should look like this.

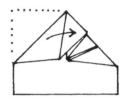

7) Now do the same to the other side. This is how it should look. (Note: these are the two front stablizers.)

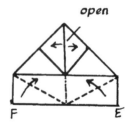

8) Now, open at the center as shown here. Fold Sides F & E diagonally up as indicated.

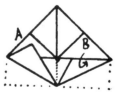

9) The folds of the lower corners should look like this. Tuck the corners under Sides A & B as shown here.

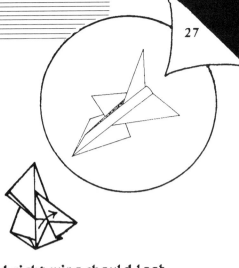

10) After you have tucked both corners under Sides A & B respectively, flip the stabilizers to the left side and make a fold on the dotted line toward the middle. Repeat on the left side.

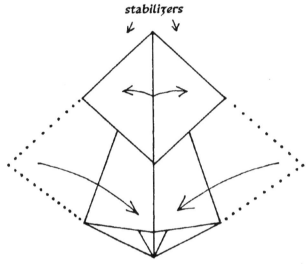

stabilizers

11) After you have folded both sides toward the middle and separated the two stabilizers, it should look like this.

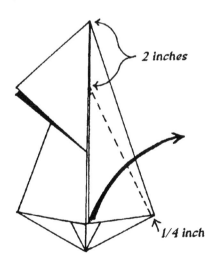

2 inches

1/4 inch

12) Fold the right wing out along the dotted line as indicated.

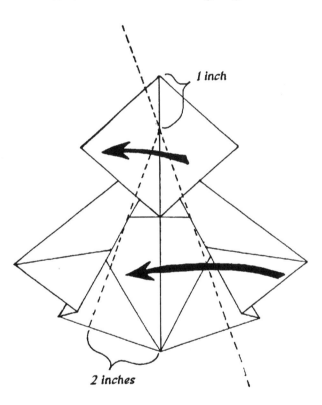

13) The folded right wing should look like this. Do the same thing on the left side before going on.

1 inch

2 inches

14) Fold the right side to the left along the dotted lines indicated by the arrows. (Note: use the technique you learned with the Concord to complete the plane.)

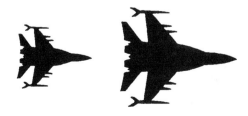

15) This is how the fold from Step 14 should look. Do the same on the left side. (Note: this new fold is great for compact planes when you don't fold the nose down first.)

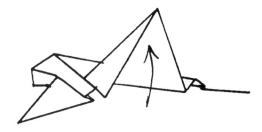

18) This is how the plane looks with the tail up.

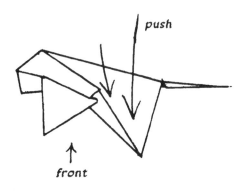

16) After you fold both sides, push the fuselage downward.

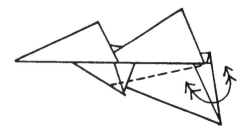

17) After you have pushed the tail down, press the two sides together. Fold the wings up, then fold the tail back and forth along the dotted lines. Now push inward and up.

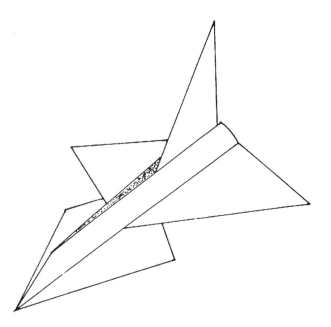

19) The finished version of the Future Fighter!

28

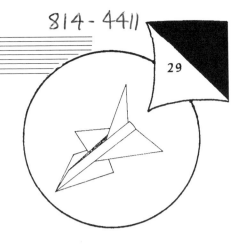

20) To make the Future Fighter plane fly, put a paperclip
underneath the nose of the plane and trim the back wing elevator up.

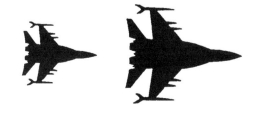

Eastern Oklahoma District Library System

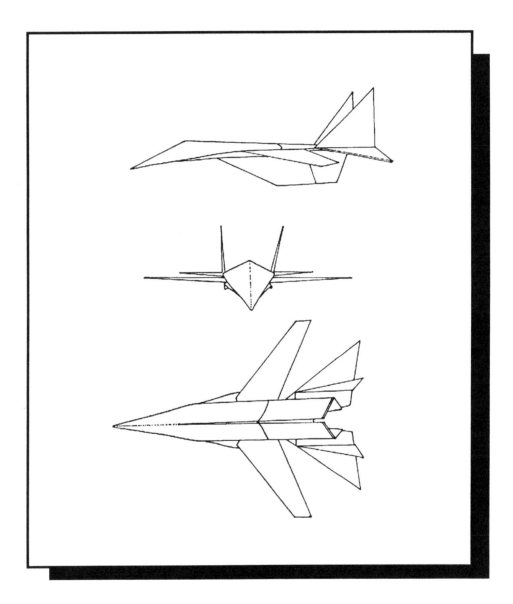

The F-15 will repeat some of the same steps and folds as the Jet, so turn back there and fold from step 1 through step 11. Then turn back here and continue.
(Note: make sure you've mastered the F-15 before folding the last plane, the F-14 Tomcat.)

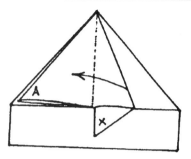

1) This is how your plane should look after you have done Steps 1-11 in the Jet section. Now, unfold & flip the right wing to the left side.

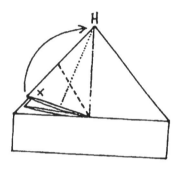

2) This is how it should look after you've flipped it to the left. Now fold on the dotted line so that Corner X meets Corner H.

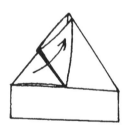

3) This is how Step 2 should look. Repeat this fold on the left side.

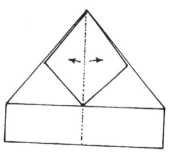

4) After you fold the left side, open both sides as indicated here.

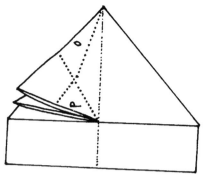

5) Now open the wings further. The front wings now have two intersecting crease lines. Label them P and O.

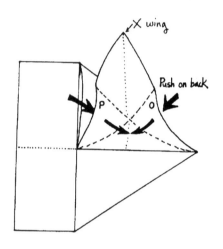

6) Rotate your paper 1/4 turn to the right and fold P & O together and toward you on the crossing crease lines.

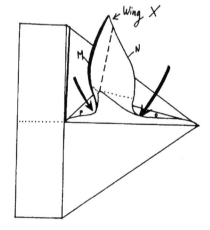

7) Your folds on P & O should look exactly as shown here. Put your hand behind the wing at M & N and press the two sides together.

32

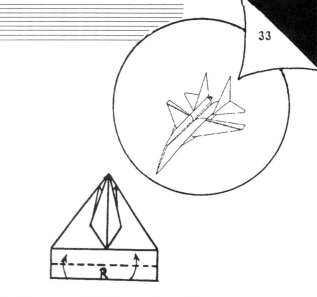

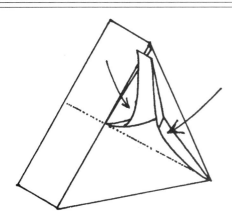

8) After pressing Sides M & N together, this is how your plane should look. Do the same on the left side, beginning with Step 5, before going on.

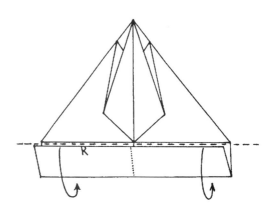

11) Fold up the R Edge at the midpoint, along the dotted line.

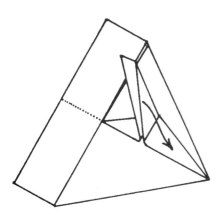

9) Your finished folds of the wing should look like this. Fold the wing up toward the nose exactly as the arrow indicates.

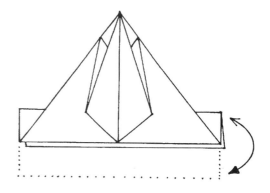

12) Now, fold back along the dotted line.

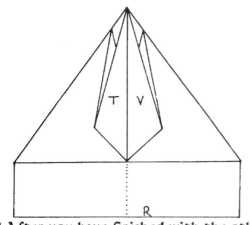

10) After you have finished with the other side, separate both sides as displayed. (Notice the R Edge.)

13) This is how your fold toward the back should look. Now unfold it as shown, so that it looks like the end of Step 11.

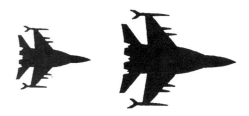

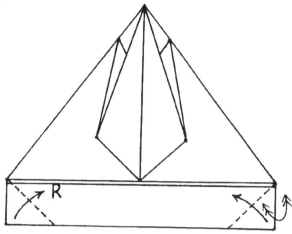

14) Fold diagonally up, then back and forth, at each corner, as shown here.

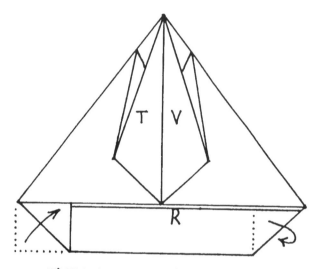

15) This is how the folds on Step 14 should look. Fold back and forth five or six times.

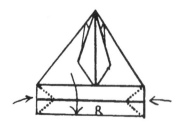

16) After you've folded the corners, unfold the R Edge fold as shown. You should have two triangular shapes.

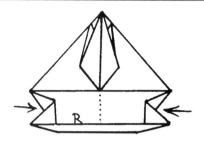

17) Push the two triangular sides inward as shown.

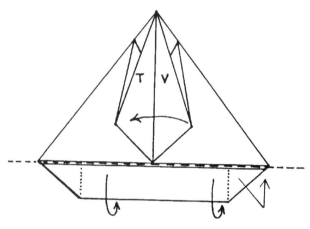

18) After you have pressed both triangular sides inward, it should look like this. Now, fold this part back on the dotted line. Next, flip the V wing to the T wing on the left side.

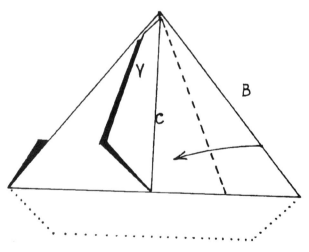

19) Now, fold Edge B to Center Line C on the dotted line. Do the same to the left side.

34

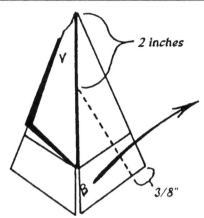

2 inches

3/8"

20) Fold Edge B to the right on the dotted line.

21) This is how your fold should look. Fold the left side the same way. Now fold the right side toward the center as shown.

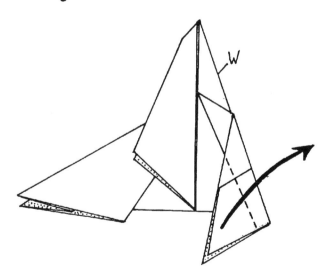

22) The fold from Step 21 should be parallel to Edge Line W. Now, make another fold on the dotted line toward the outside.

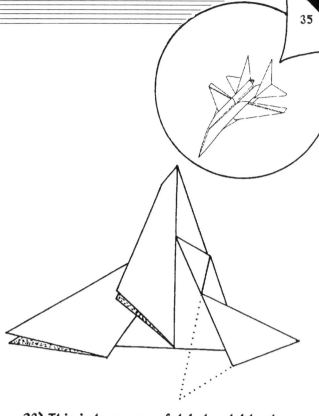

23) This is how your fold should look.

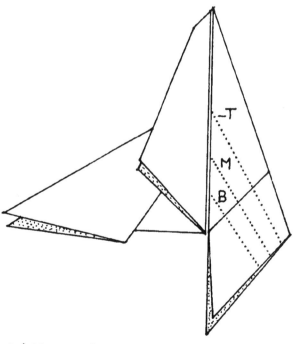

24) Now, unfold the wing as shown here. You should have three crease lines, T, M & B, in the middle.

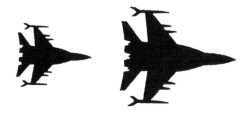

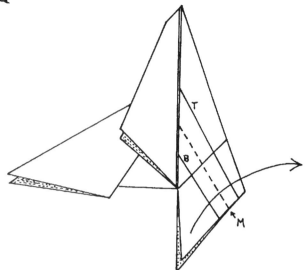

25) Hold the paper straight; fold toward the outside along dotted crease Line M.

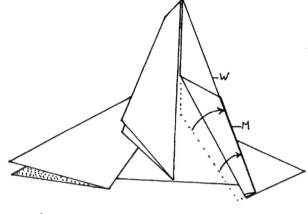

28) Repeat Steps 21-27 for the left side.

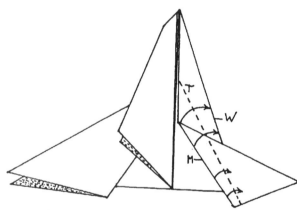

26) Your fold should look like this. Again, fold Edge M to Edge W.

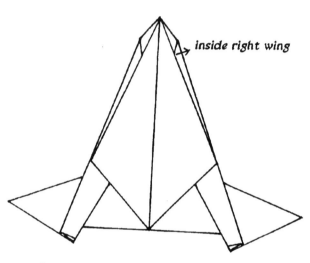

29) Now, separate the two front wings so that the plane looks like this.

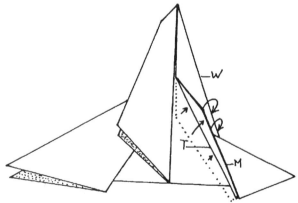

27) This is how the fold from Step 26 should look.

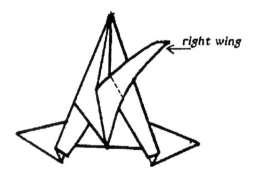

30) Fold the inside right wing to match the angle of the right stabilizer (see Step 31). Do the same to the inside left wing.

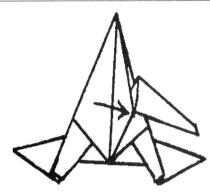

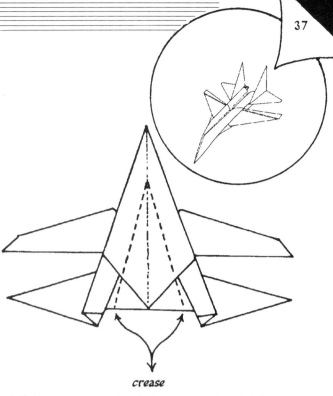

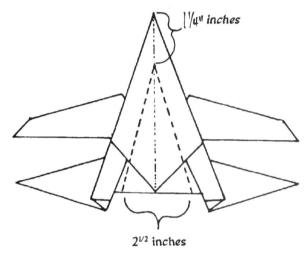

31) Match the angle of the front wing to the stabilizer. Do the same to the other side.

1¼" inches

2½ inches

32) This is what your plane should look like.

crease

34) Now, open the folds; you should have two crease lines.

push down

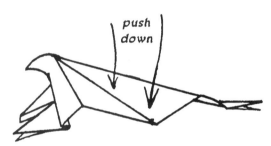

35) After you have folded the two sides, you should be able to push the belly downward without losing the sharp nose.

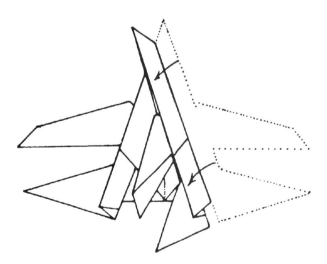

33) Now, fold the right side to the left and fold the left side to the right.

36) After you have pushed the belly down, lift up the two tail fins.

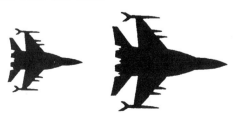

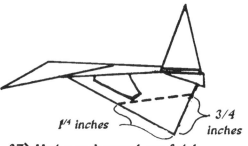

1¼ inches   3/4 inches

37) Make an inward-up fold
of about 1/2 inch.

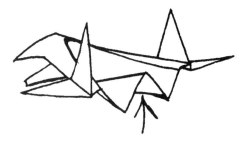

38) From the rear, the plane should look
like this.

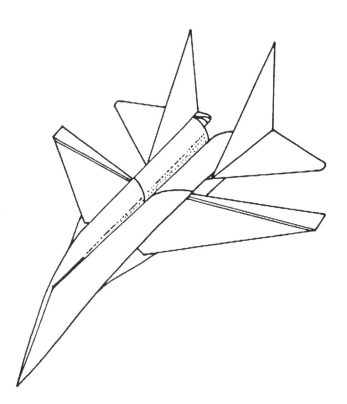

39) The finished version of the F-15!

40) Due to its compact shape, this wonderful plane will not fly as well as the others. But it's ideal for collectors. If you wish to fly it add weight to the nose and trim the elevators up.

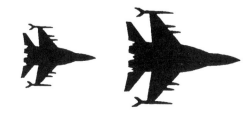

STEALTH

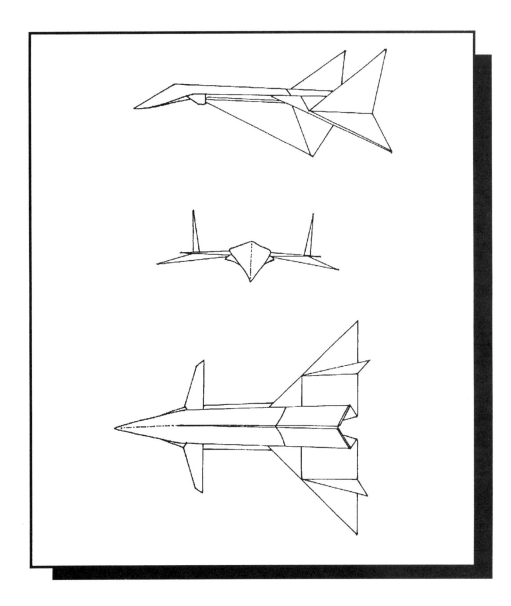

To make the Stealth, repeat Steps 1-11 from the Jet. Then turn to the F-15 and repeat Steps 1-20. Then come back here and continue.

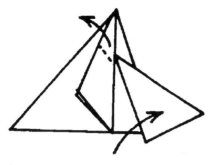

1) After repeating Steps 1-11 from the Jet and Steps 1-20 from the F-15, your plane should look like this. Fold the front stabilizer straight to the left side as shown by the top arrow. (Note: the left side has not been folded toward the middle in this drawing.)

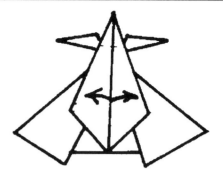

4) After you've finished both sides, separate them as shown.

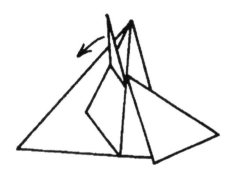

2) This is how the fold should look.

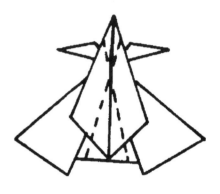

5) Fold on the dotted lines, as indicated. Fold the right side to the left and the left side to the right exactly as on the F-15. (Note: work on a flat surface.)

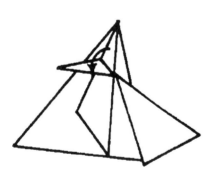

3) This is how your fully folded stabilizer should look. Flip the right stabilizer to the right and do the same on the other side.

6) This is how your fold to the left side should look. Press hard on the fold, then unfold it and do the same on the left side.

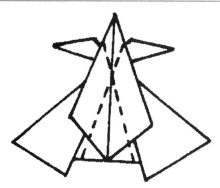

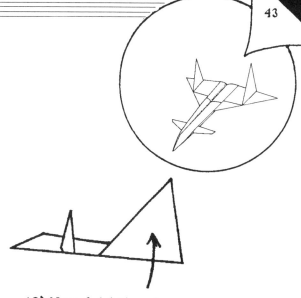

7) After you've folded the two sides of the plane, open it up. You should see two crease lines (as shown by the dotted lines.)

10) Now fold the wings up.

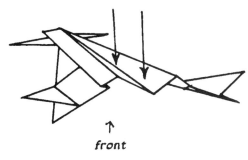

front

8) Now, turn your plane over, with the belly down. Press the center line down as indicated by the arrows until the two sides come close together. With your thumb and fingers, press the plane's fuselage tightly together.

11) Fold up the two tail wings as shown.

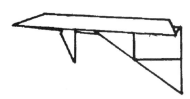

9) This is how your plane should look from the side.

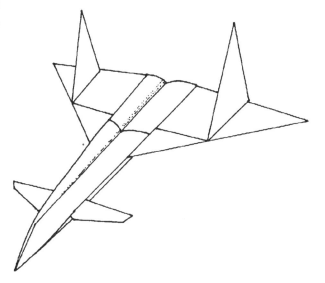

12) The finished version of the Stealth!

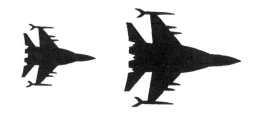

13) This plane is similar to the F-15 (compact), so it is not a good flyer.
(If you wish to fly it, add weight to the nose and trim the elevators upward.)

44

BOMBER

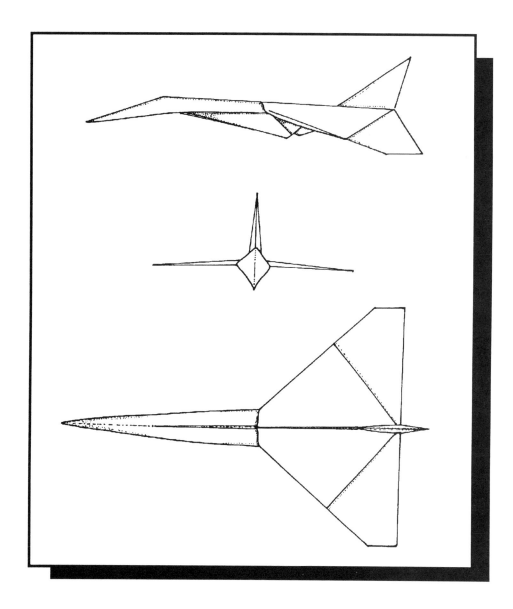

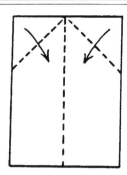

1) Fold the paper in half. Then open it and fold the two top corners toward the center line.

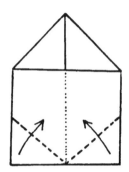

2) This is how your folds should look. Now make the bottom folds at the corners, as indicated.

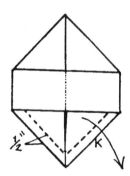

3) This is how the folds on the four corners should look. Make a downward-out fold as indicated, leaving about 1/2 inch.

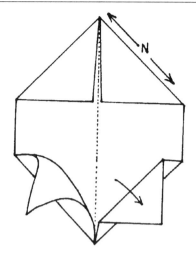

4) This is how your downward-out fold should look.

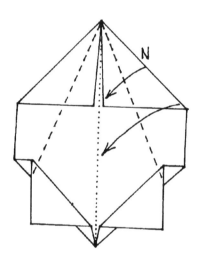

5) Now, fold Edge N on the dotted line to the center line.

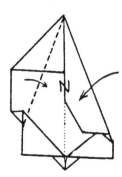

6) This is how your N Line fold toward the center line should look. Do the same to the other side.

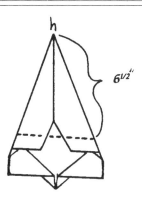

7) The plane should now look like this. Next, measure 6$^{1/2}$ inches from H and fold down along the dotted line.

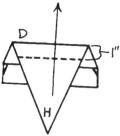

8) This is how the fold should look. Now, fold up on the dotted line, which should be about 1 inch from Line D.

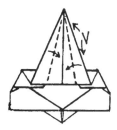

9) Now the plane should look like this. Fold Edge V to the center line.

10) This is how your fold toward the center line should look. Open it back up and do the same on the other side.

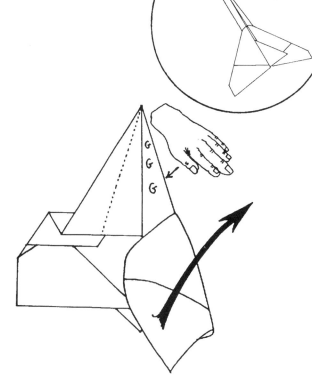

11) After you open it up again, close it and put your left hand over the G spots and open the lower part of the wing with your right hand.

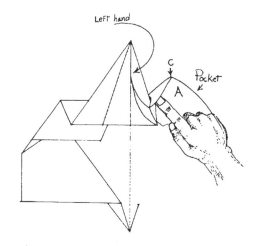

12) You should be able to spot a pocket where you see the A. Stick your finger in as shown and place your left thumb above the pocket where the C is shown.

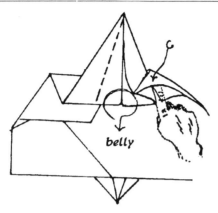

13) Gently, press down from the top of the pocket; it should close easily.

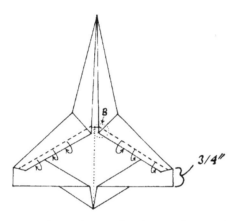

14) After pressing down both pockets, the plane should look like this. (Notice the 3/4" wing edge.) Fold the indicated edges under the wings and belly as shown by the arrows.

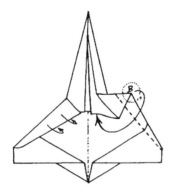

15) The B corner should be folded directly under the belly. It should look exactly like the left finished side on the diagram. This is a very important step.

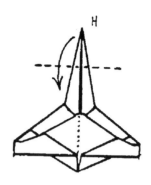

16) After you have folded the two parts under the belly, your plane should look exactly as shown. Now, $2^{1/2}$ inches down from H, fold along the dotted line.

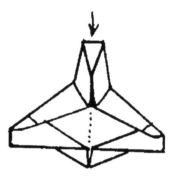

17) This is how your fold should look.

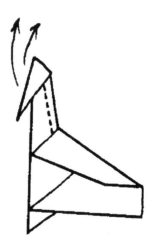

18) After you have folded the nose down, fold the two sides of the plane toward the back so that it looks like this from the side view. Then, lift up the nose.

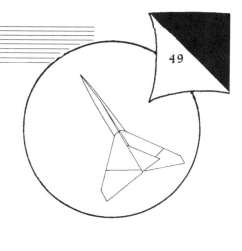

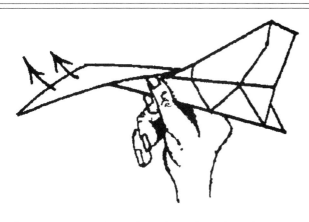

19) Hold your right hand under the plane as shown and, with your left hand, pull up the nose of the plane.

20) After you have pulled up the nose, carefully line up the plane's back so that it looks exactly as shown here.

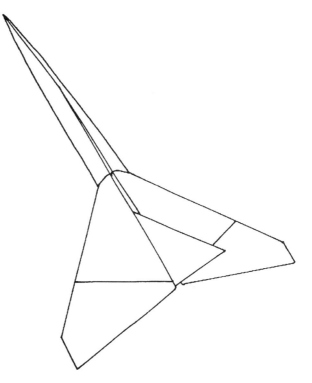

22) The finished version of the Bomber!

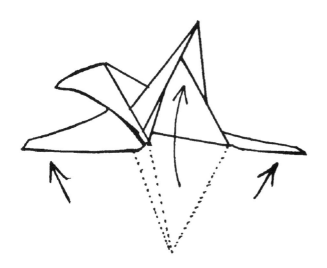

21) Now, lift up the plane's wings so that they are flat and even. Then lift the tail fin as indicated. Fold the wings back down and press hard on them from both sides of the fuselage. Finally, lift the wings up again and you're done.

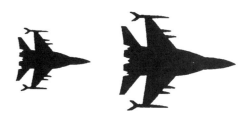

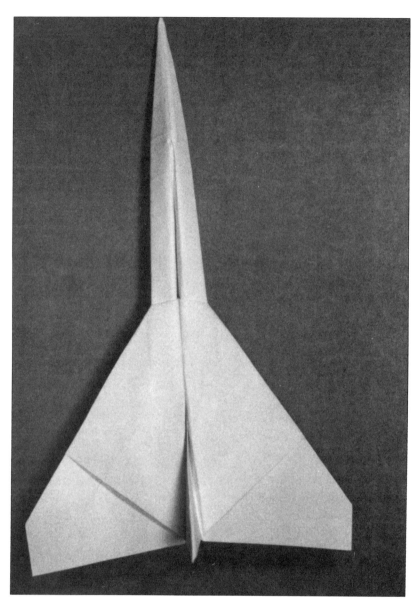

23) Throw this plane straight out from your body and it should fly smoothly.

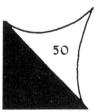

STAR FIGHTER

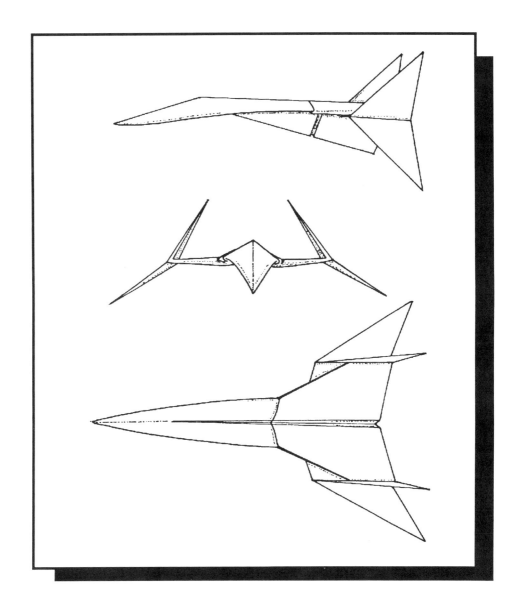

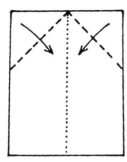

1) Fold the paper in half and open it back up. Fold the top two corners toward the middle line.

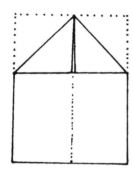

2) Your folds should look like this.

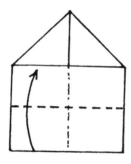

3) Fold up along the dotted line.

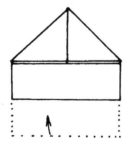

4) Your fold should look like this

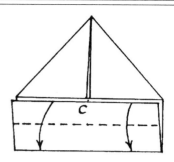

5) Fold down Edge C at the midpoint.

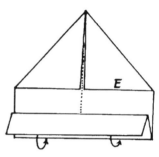

6A) Your fold should look like this.

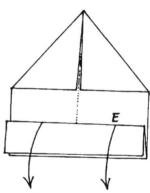

6B) Unfold Edge E.

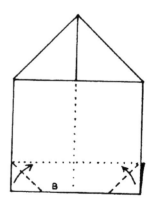

7) Make two upward folds from the two bottom corners as shown, along the diagonal dotted lines.

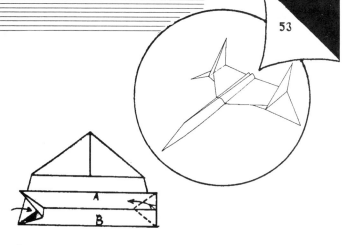

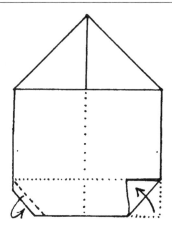

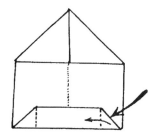

8) This is how your bottom corner folds should look. Fold back and forth four to five times at each corner.

11) Lift Edge A halfway up, as shown. Now you should have a triangular shape on each side. Push both triangular shapes inward and toward each other.

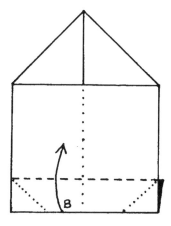

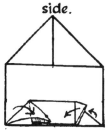

9) Open the corners as shown. Then fold the bottom edge line B upward, along the dotted line.

12) This is how it should look. Now fold the right fin as indicated to the left side on the dotted line. Do the same on the left side.

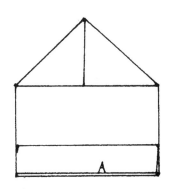

10) Your fold should look like this.

13) Your fold to the center should look like this.

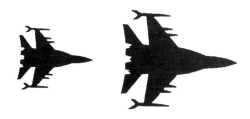

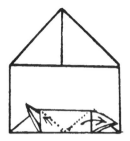

14) Now, unfold to the outside as indicated.

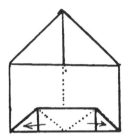

15) After you have completed the folds toward the outside, you should have this.

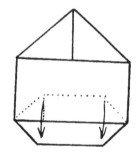

16) Unfold down as shown.

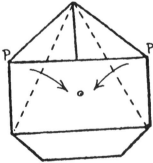

17) Fold the two P corners as shown along the dotted lines toward the center line.

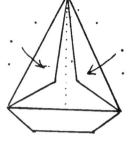

18) After you fold the two sides inward, your plane should look like this.

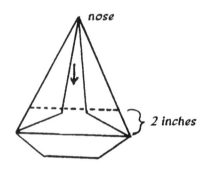

19) Fold the nose down along the dotted line.

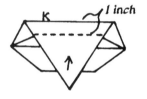

20) Now fold up along the dotted line, as shown.

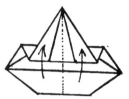

21) Your fold should look like this.

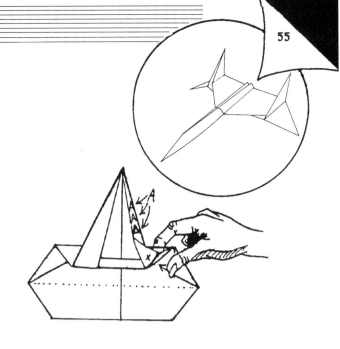

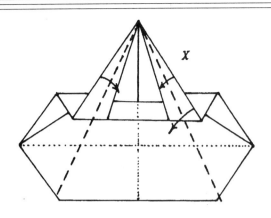

22) Now fold Edge X toward the center line. (Note: the intent of this fold is to get two triangular shapes in Step 26.)

23) This is how your fold should look. Now unfold it and repeat on the other side.

25) Simply place your left hand over the A's while your right finger and thumb press the pocket downward to look like Step 26.

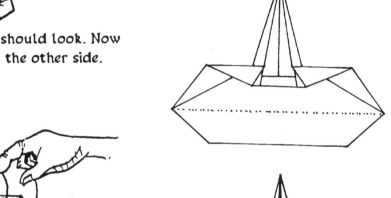

24) After you have unfolded the sides, you should have a little pocket behind the X. Put your index finger inside and your thumb on the X, as indicated by the arrows.

26) You should now have two upside-down triangular shapes. Yours may look a bit different, but carry on.

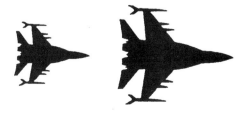

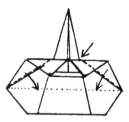

27) Now, fold both sides diagonally down as shown, along the dotted lines.

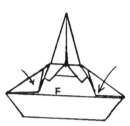

28) This is how the folds should look.

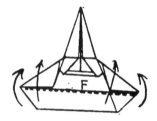

29) Fold up the lower part along dotted Line F.

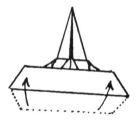

30) This is how your fold should look.

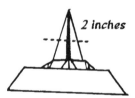

31) Now, fold the nose down along the dotted line (about two inches down).

32) This is how your fold should look. Now fold the whole plane back and together, in half.

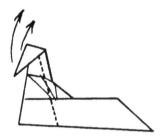

33) This is how the fold toward the back should look from the side. Next, lift up the nose and pinch along the belly about one inch up. (Note: For the best results, always place the plane's back against a flat surface.)

34) This is how the plane should look after you've lifted the nose and aligned the fuselage. The tiny Line M should be about 1/4 inch long.

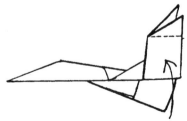

35) Now, lift up the wings as shown.

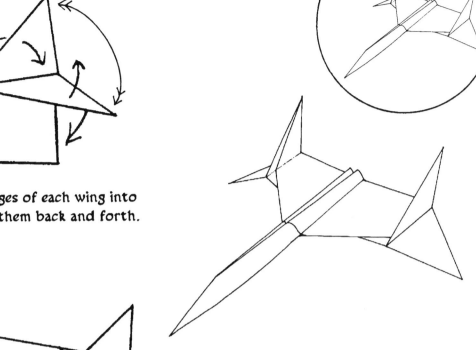

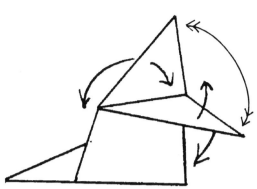

36) Separate the edges of each wing into two sides and fold them back and forth.

37) This is how your plane should look.

39) The finished version of the Star Fighter!

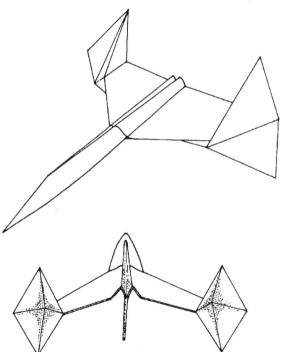

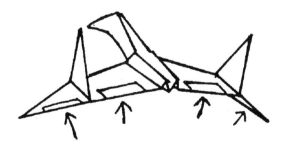

38) Trim up at the arrows for good lift. (Option: make cuts for flaps for easier flying.)

40) You can also open the tail fins to make the rocket boosters appear.

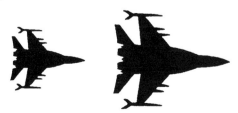

STEALTH FIGHTER

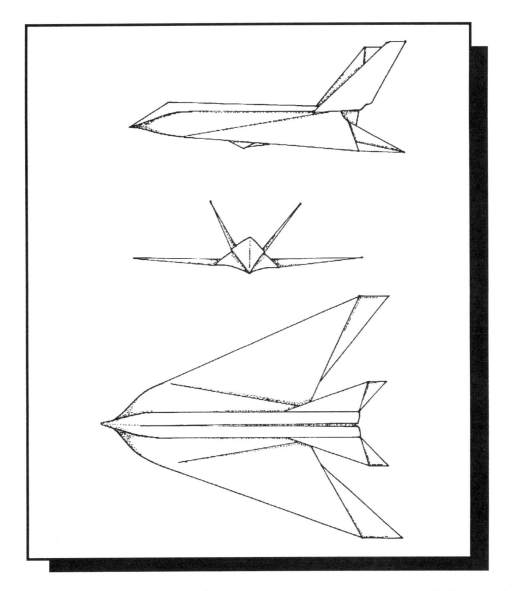

In making the Stealth Fighter, be careful and precise when you tear and tuck the wing inward.
(Note: this technique will also be necessary for the Mig-27.)

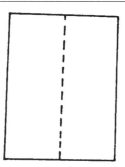

1) Fold the paper in half, then open it back up.

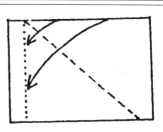

5) Turn your paper sideways. Fold the top right corner diagonally down to the left crease line as indicated.

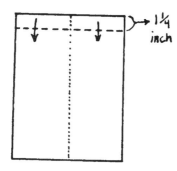

1¼ inch

2) Fold it down about 1¹′⁴″ from the top.

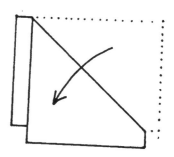

6) Fold from the top right corner.

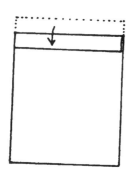

3) Your fold should look like this.

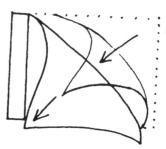

7) It should look like this.

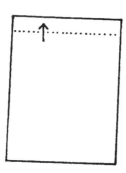

4) Open it back up.

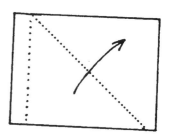

8) Now, open it back up.

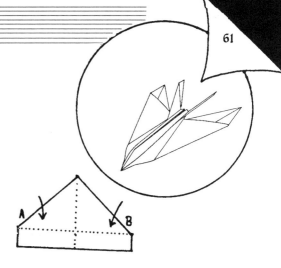

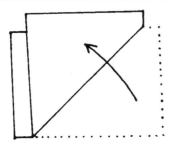

9) Make a fold from the lower right hand corner diagonally up and left as shown.

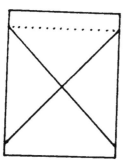

10) Open it back up, rotate your paper a quarter turn and you should have the crossing lines you see here.

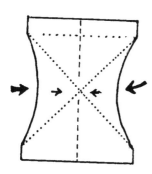

11) Fold the sides inward.

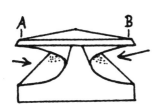

12) Your inward fold should look like this.

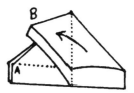

13) Press down and it should look like this. The base might not be even, but don't worry about it.

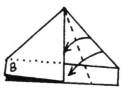

14) Flip Fin B to the left side.

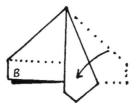

15) Make a fold toward the middle line as shown by the arrows.

16) Your fold should look like this.

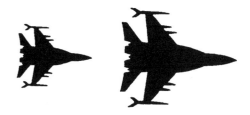

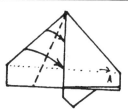

17) Do the same on the left side.

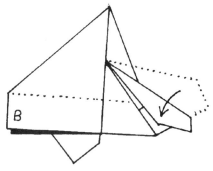

21) Your fold should look like this.
Do the same on the left side.

2³/⁴ inches

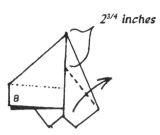

18) Flip Flaps A & B to the left.
Fold outward along the dotted line.

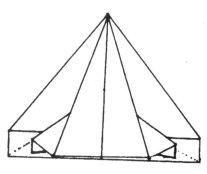

back side

22) Now, turn the paper over so that you
can see how the back looks.

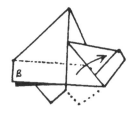

19) Your fold should look like this.

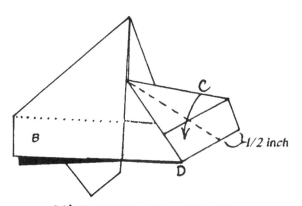

C

B

1/2 inch

D

20) Fold Edge C to Edge D.

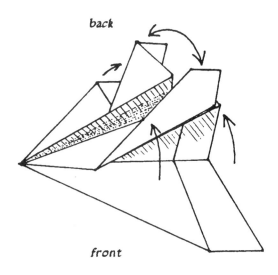

back

front

23) Raise the two folded sides
and make sure they're even.

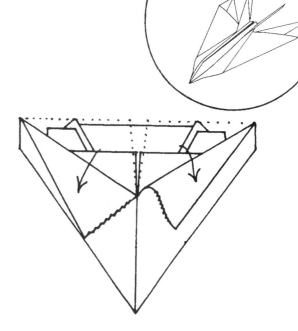

front

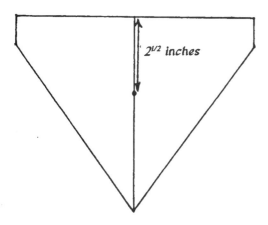

2¹⁄² inches

24) Turn the plane over and make a tear about 2¹⁄² inches long as indicated here.

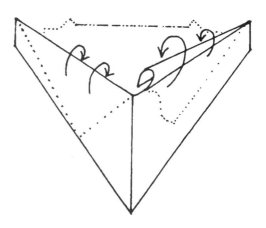

26) The folds should look like this.

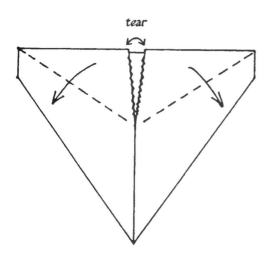

tear

25) Your tear should look like this. Fold the two sides as indicated. (Note: cutting is optional.)

27) Now, fold the two flaps inward under the wings.

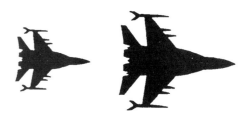

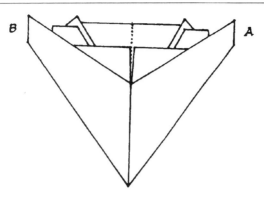

28) Now the plane should look like this.

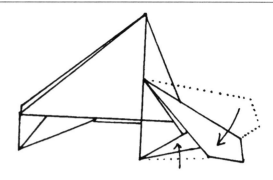

31) Now, fold the upper portion of the tail fin down. Do the same on the other side.

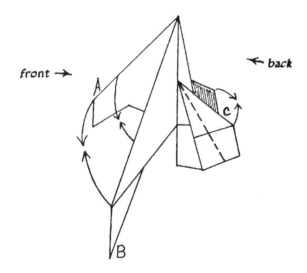

29) Stand the paper upright and fold Sides A & B to the left and the two small sides to the right, so that it looks like this. Unfold the C Edges.

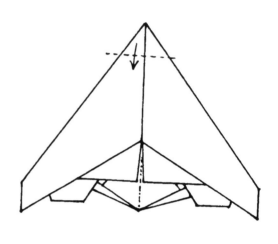

32) Now spread the plane open. It should look like this.

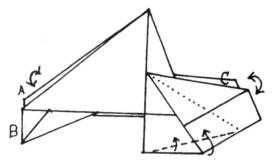

30) Your plane should look like this. Make a small fold up on the bottom as indicated, on the top flap only. Do the same on the other side.

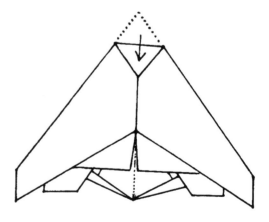

33) Fold the nose down toward you about one inch from the top.

64

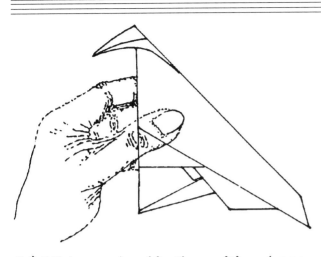

34) With your hand in the position shown,
turn the plane sideways.
(Note: remember this procedure
from previous airplanes.)

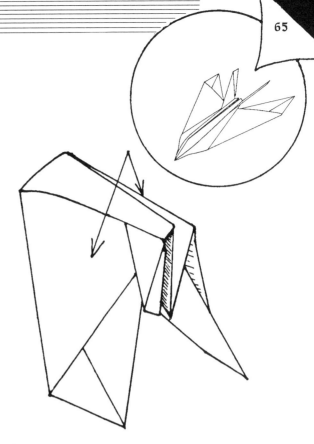

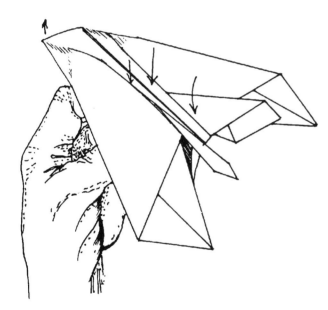

35) Now, grip the belly with your left hand
and use your right hand to line up the back,
then press the two sides down, as shown
in this top view.

36) This is how your plane should look
after you have folded the two sides down.

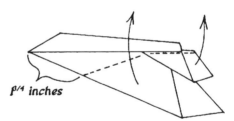

ⁱ/4 inches

37A) Fold along the dotted line for
a more authentic looking plane.

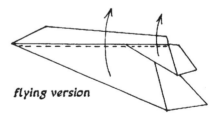

flying version

37B) From the side, your plane should now
look like this. Fold the wings up as
indicated & do the same on the other side.

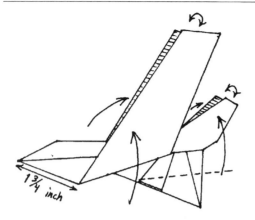

38) This is how the plane should look after you have folded the four wings up. Make sure they're even.

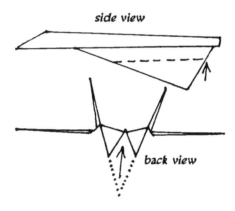

side view

back view

39) Make an inward-up fold as indicated, similar to the ones you have made on earlier planes in this book.

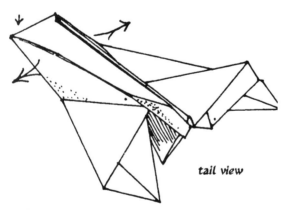

tail view

40) Lift up and widen the two sides as indicated by the arrows.

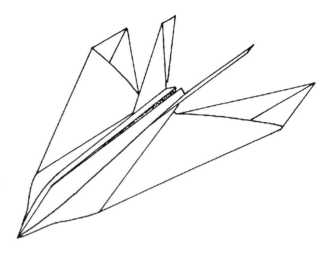

41) The finished version of the Stealth Fighter!

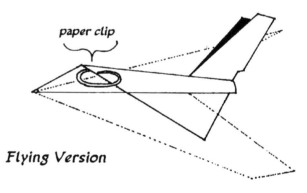

paper clip

Flying Version

42) To fly this plane, place a paper clip as shown, and tightly press the nose to make it pointed. Slide the paper clip back & forth for balance. Throw the plane straight out from your body & it should fly and glide smoothly.

66

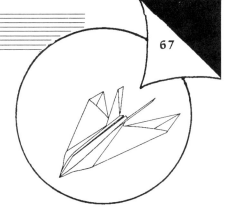

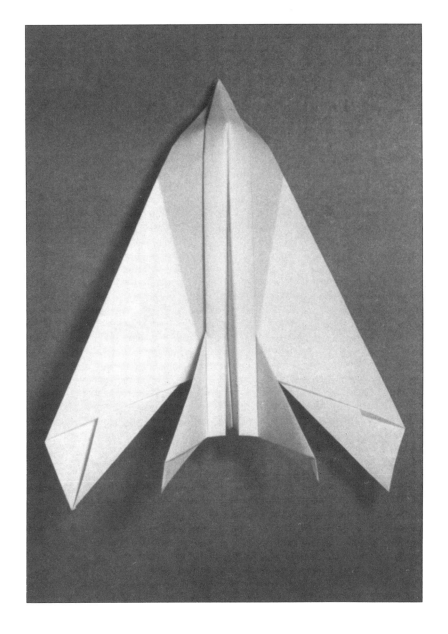

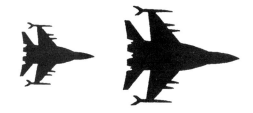

MIG-27

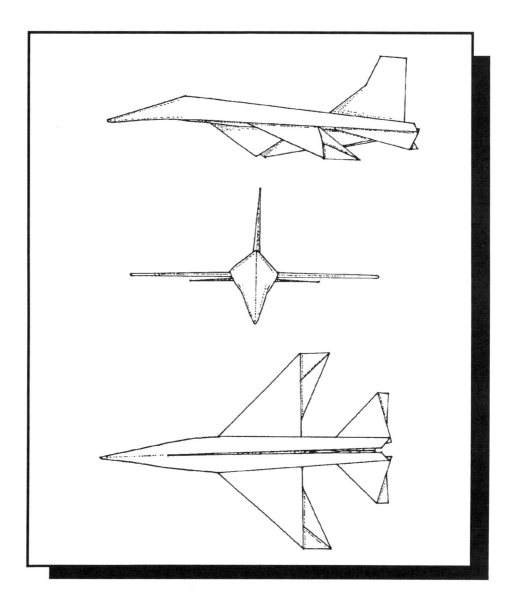

You will not be able to make this plane until you have mastered both the Stealth Fighter and the Jet. In making the Mig-27, after a few initial folds, you'll need to repeat some steps from the Stealth Fighter and a few steps from the Jet, as indicated.

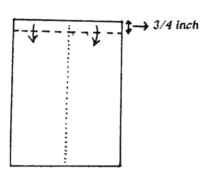

→ 3/4 inch

1) Fold the paper in half, open it back up, and fold the top part down 3/4 inch.

2) Now, turn back to the Stealth Fighter section and do Steps 4 through 13. Then proceed to Step 3 on this page.

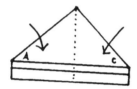

3) Your plane should now look like this.

4) Turn back to Step 13 of the Stealth Fighter and fold through Step 16. Then come back here and proceed with Step 5.

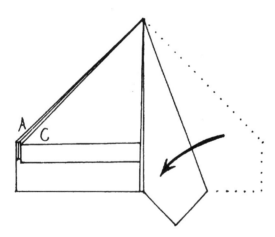

5) Your plane should now look like this.

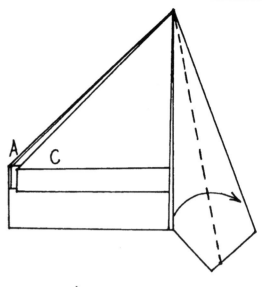

6) Fold as indicated.

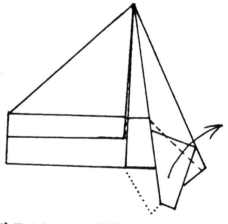

7) Fold the stabilizer out as shown.

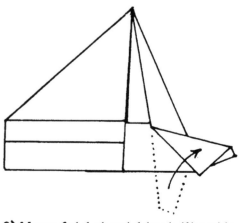

8) Your fold should look like this.

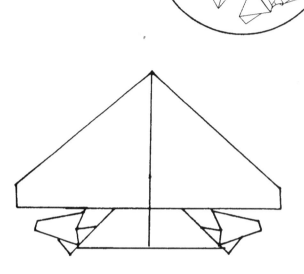

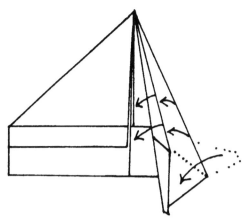

9) Unfold the side as shown.

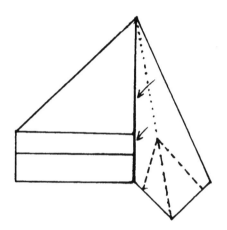

10) Your plane should now look like this.

11) Now, turn to Step 33 in the Jet section and fold from there through Step 36. Then turn back here and continue with Step 12.

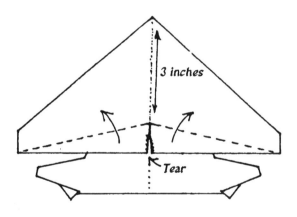

13) Open up the plane so it looks like this.

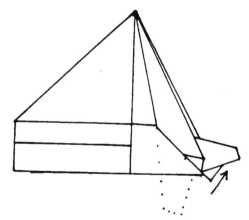

12) Your inward-out fold should look like this. Repeat Steps 5-12 on the left side.

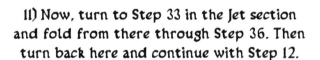

3 inches

Tear

14) Make a tear (as you did with the Stealth). Like the Stealth Fighter, fold toward the inside.

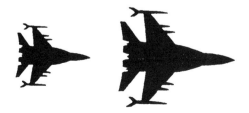

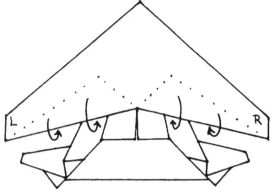

15) Your inside fold should look like this. (Notice the L left wing & R right wing.)

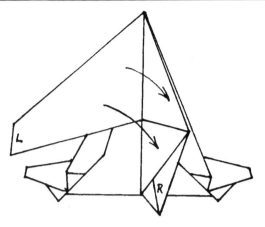

18) Flip Wing R to the right as shown one more time.

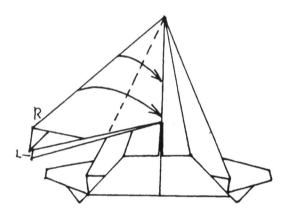

16) Fold the R wing toward the middle line.

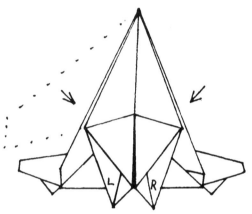

19) Make the same fold on the left side. It should look like this.

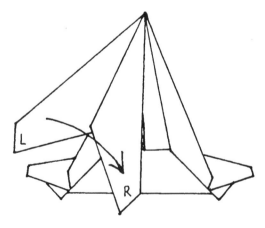

17) Your fold should look like this.

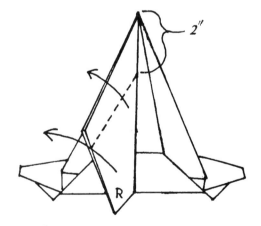

20) Fold the R wing to the left, then fold again along the dotted line.

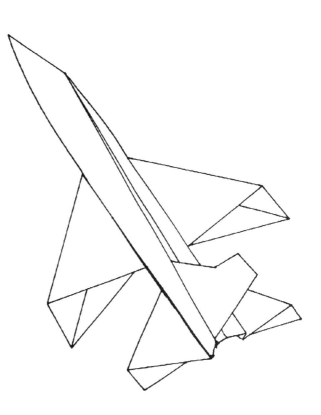

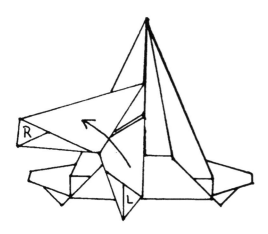

21) Your R right wing fold should look like
this. Do the same on the L left wing.

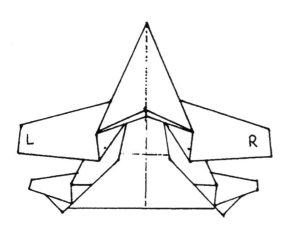

22) Open the R wing to the right side, L to
the left and you should have this. Now,
fold the nose down and finish the plane. If
you have trouble, go on to the next step.

23) Now turn back to the Jet section and,
starting with Step 37, continue to the end.
(Note: don't forget to cut the tail if you
want to make it look more realistic.)
Your finished version should look like this.

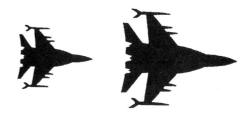

25) Fly this plane the same way you would fly the Jet.

74

VIGGEN

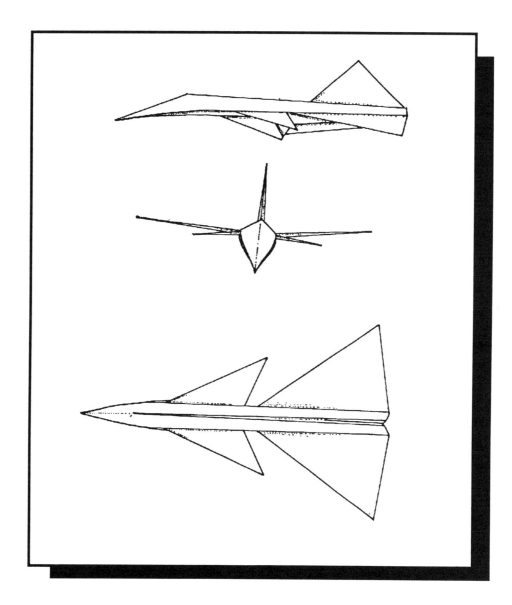

To make the Viggen Fighter, turn back to the Jet section,
and fold from Step 1 through Step 8. Then come back here.

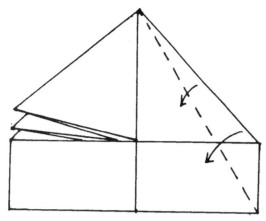

1) After you have completed Steps 1-8 in the Jet section, your plane should look like this. Make a fold on the dotted line.

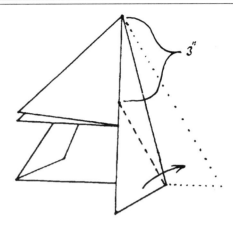

4) Make another fold along the dotted line.

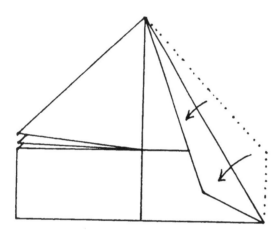

2) Your fold should look like this.

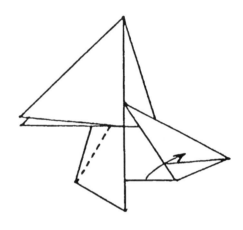

5) Your fold out should look like this. Do the same on the left side.

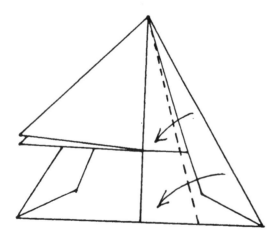

3) Make a fold to the center along the dotted line.

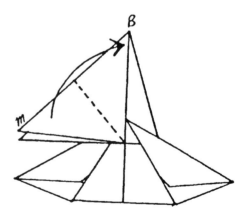

6) Fold up along the dotted line to the tip.

76

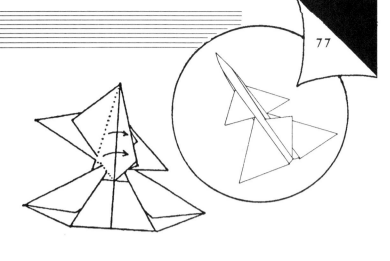

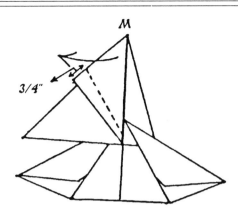

7) Now fold to the left on the dotted line.

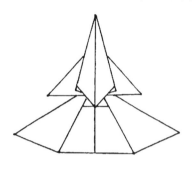

10) Your completed fold of the K Edge should turn out like this.

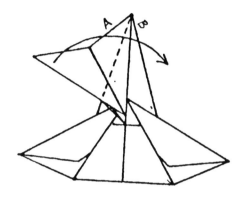

8) Your fold to the left side should look like this. Repeat Steps 6 & 7 to the left side. (Fold Edge A to the right, even with Edge B.)

12) Now, repeat Steps 8, 9, 10 & 11 on the left side, and then separate the sides. It should look like this.

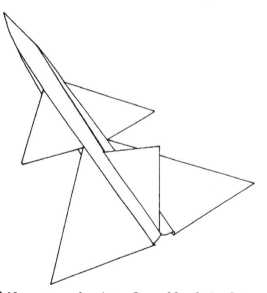

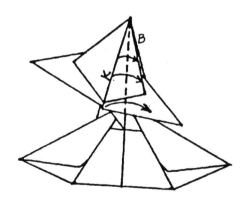

9) Your fold to the right should look like this. Now fold Edge K to the right so it's even with Edge B.

12) Now, turn back to Step 38 of the Jet and finish making the body as shown there. Your finished version should look like this.

13) Fly this plane the same way as the Jet.

HORNET F-18

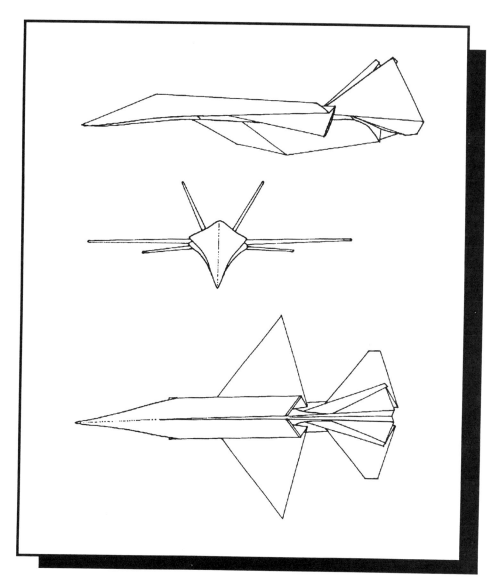

This is the U.S. F-18 Hornet, a unique fighter. The Hornet cannot be folded until you have mastered the Jet and the planes that follow. Additionally, you should be comfortable making an even-opposite fold each time you see one in a diagram, folding down the nose of a plane and pushing its tail inward-up. (All these steps are used in the construction of previous planes in this book.) Like the real Hornet on which this plane is modeled, it will fly straight and fast. It's a tough plane, so be patient; you can ensure a compact and sturdy shape by making sure the folds are tight and accurate.

Now turn back to the Jet section and follow Steps 1 through 13. Then turn back here; your plane should look exactly as shown in the first diagram on the next page.

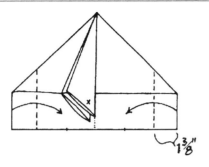

1) Measure about 1³/₈ inches in at each side;
fold toward the middle
as indicated by the arrows.

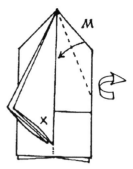

5) Turn the model over and flip the wings
(A & X) onto the left side;
fold Edge M toward the center.

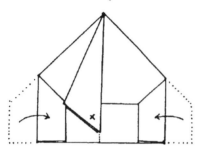

2) Your folds should look like this.
(Note: back sides are Wings A & X.)

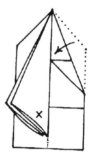

6) It should look like this.
Do the same on the left side.

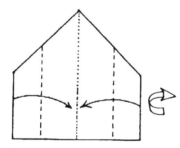

3) Turn the model over.
Fold each side in toward the middle.

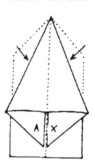

7) This is what you should have
after completing Steps 5 & 6 and
separating the two wings.

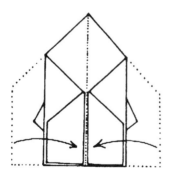

4) Your plane should look like this.

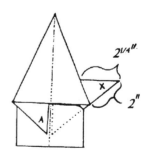

8) Pull the wings out (using the technique
learned on earlier planes).
Do the same to the left side.

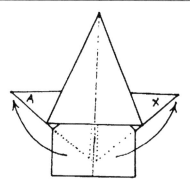

9) Now your plane should look like this.

Front of plane

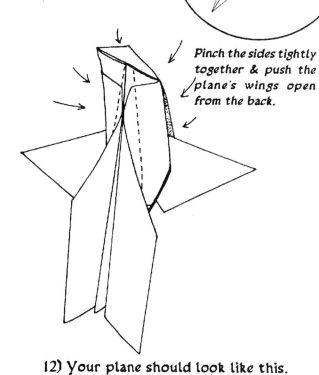

Pinch the sides tightly
together & push the
plane's wings open
from the back.

10) Turn the plane over; it will look like
this. (The back now becomes the front.)

12) Your plane should look like this.

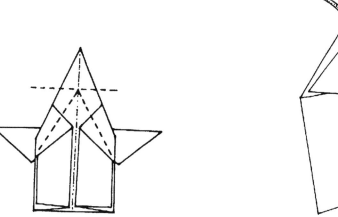

11) Fold the nose down and both sides of
the body together. (You should remember
how from previous planes.)

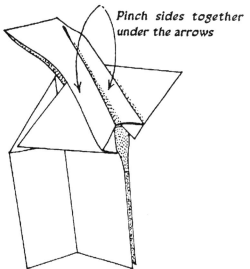

Pinch sides together
under the arrows

13) Your plane should look like this.

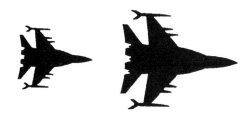

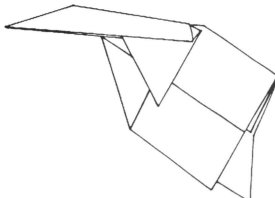

14) Side view.

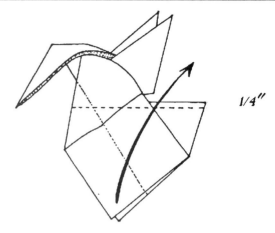

1/4"

17) Now, open up the wings and fold as indicated. Do one side first, then the other.

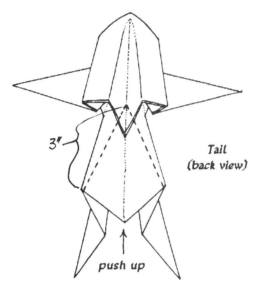

3"

Tail
(back view)

push up

15) Tail (back view). Push up, as you've done with the tail fins of previous planes.

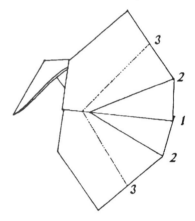

3
2
1
2
3

18) Your plane should look like this. Do the same on the other side. (Notice the 3 crease lines)

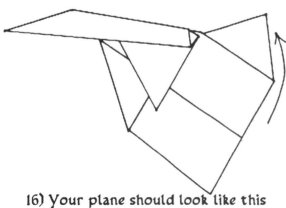

16) Your plane should look like this

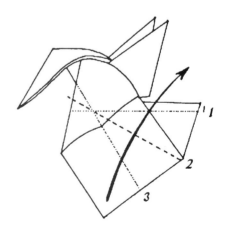

1
2
3

19) Unfold and fold again, so that Crease Line 3 is directly on Crease Line 1.

82

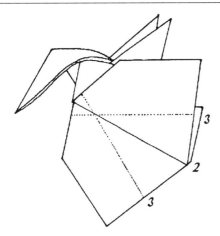

20) Your fold should look like this.
Do the same on the other side.

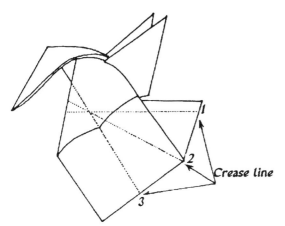

21) Unfold it and, as in step 18, you
should have 3 crease lines.

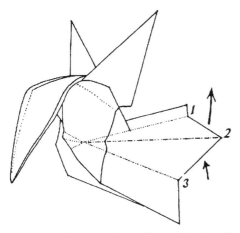

22) Push up Crease Line 2 and bring Crease
Lines 1 & 3 together (the same way you
would push up the tail).

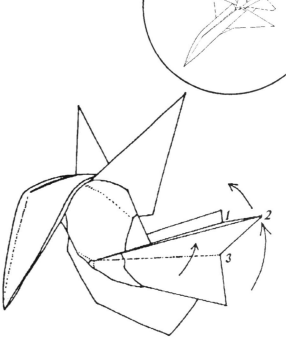

23) Your plane should look like this.
Repeat Steps 21 & 22 on the other side.

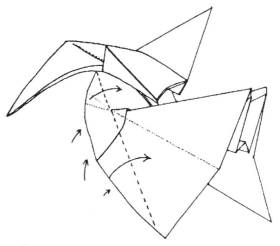

24) As you bring up the tail fin, the side
shown here will collapse inward.
Carefully fold it inward along the
dotted line, as indicated by the arrows.
Do the same to the other side.

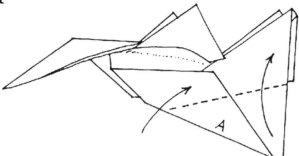

25) Your plane should look exactly like this. Fold the stabilizers up. Make sure you duplicate this pattern on both sides.

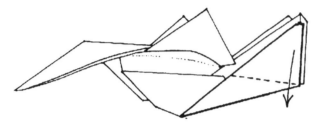

26) Now, fold the stabilizers down. Do the same on the other side.

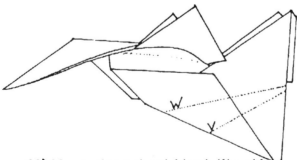

27) Open the stabilizers down completely.

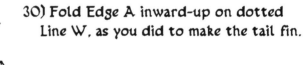

28) Your plane should look like this. Crease Lines V & W should be visible.

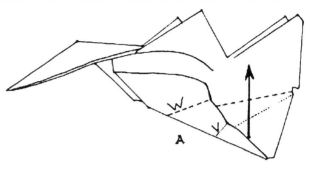

29) Using the inward-up folding techniques you learned when folding the Jet's tail stabilizers and tail fins, fold the tail inward and up on Crease Line V.

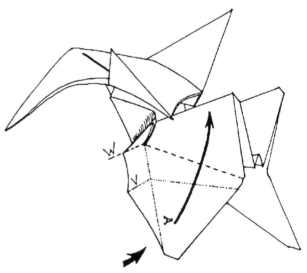

30) Fold Edge A inward-up on dotted Line W, as you did to make the tail fin.

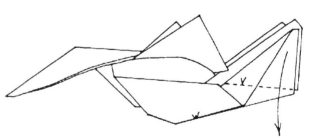

31) Your plane should look like this. Fold the stabilizers down. Repeat on the other side.

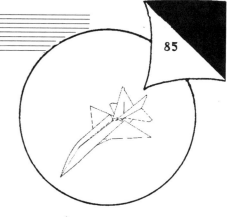

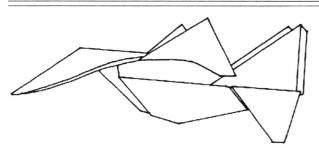

32) Your plane should look like this.

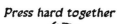

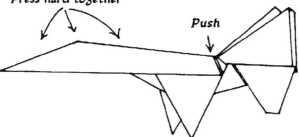

Press hard together

Push

33) Press the body tightly together.
Push down at the tail joint
to separate the two tails.

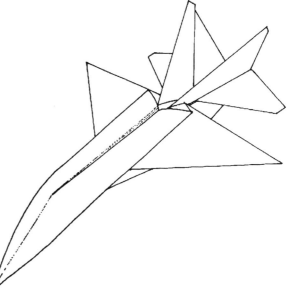

35) The finished version of the Hornet F-18!

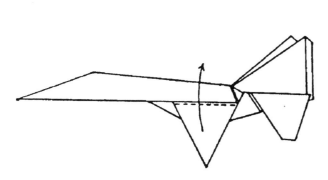

34) Fold the wings up.

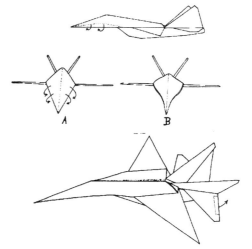

36) Curve the side of the nose for a nice,
round, clean, front end like the one in
Diagram B.

LASER-JET

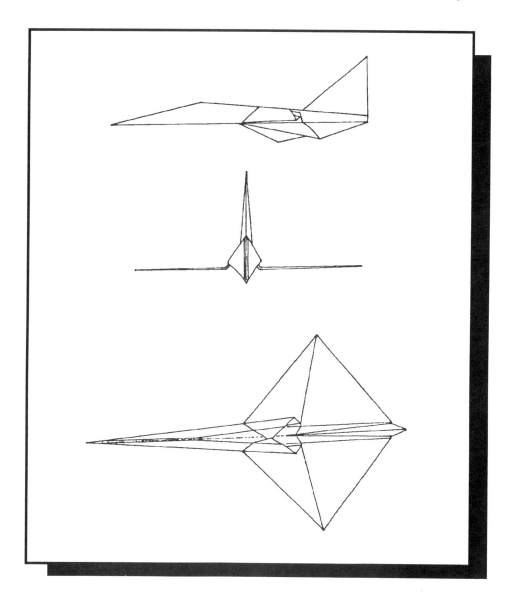

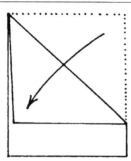

1) Fold a sheet of paper as shown.

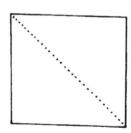

2) Your paper should look like this. Cut off, or fold from side to side on the dotted line and tear off.

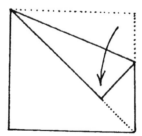

3) Your should now have this square shape with a diagonal crease line.

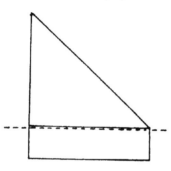

4) Fold the top right corner down. Do the same to the left corner.

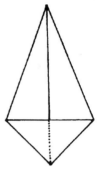

5) Your plane should look like this.

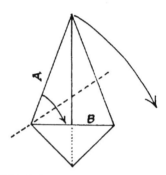

6) Fold on the dotted line, bringing Edge A over Line B.

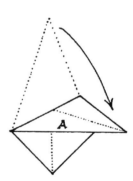

7) This is the way the fold should look.

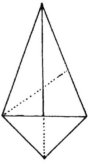

8) Unfold it and do the same on the other side.

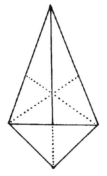

9) You should have two intersecting crease lines.

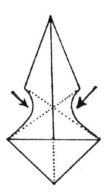

10) Make an inward fold on the sides and fold the tip down (as in previous planes).

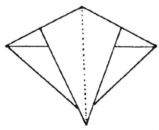

11) Your fold should look like this.

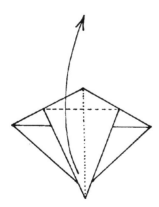

12) Fold the tip back up on the dotted line.

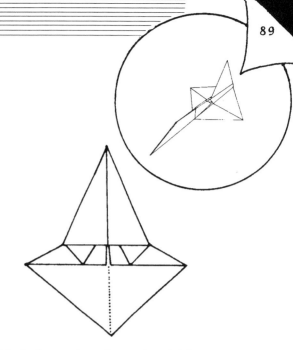

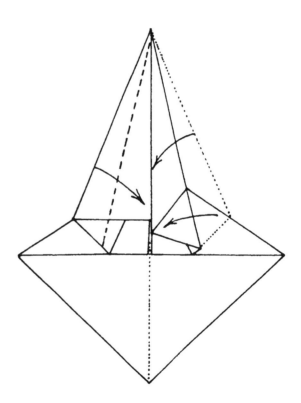

13) This is how the plane should look now.

14) Fold the right side to the center as shown. Do the same on the left side.

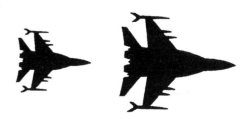

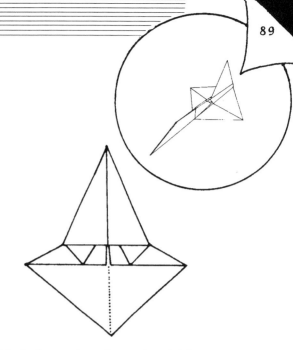

89

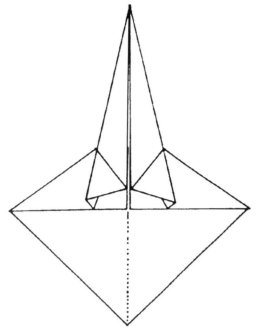

15) This is how your plane should look.

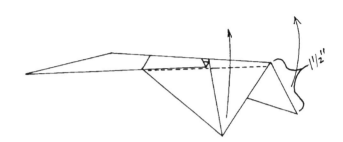

17) From the side, your plane should look like this. Fold the wings and the tail fin up.

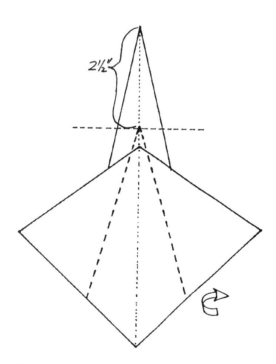

2½"

16) Turn the plane over. Fold the nose down and proceed to align the back as you have with previous planes.

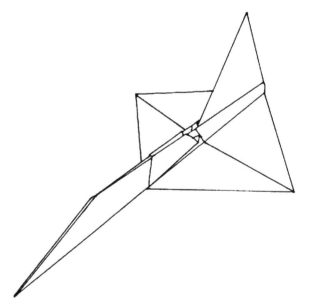

18) The finished version of the Laser Jet!

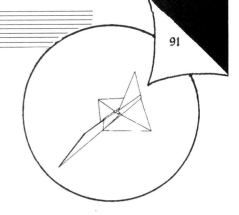

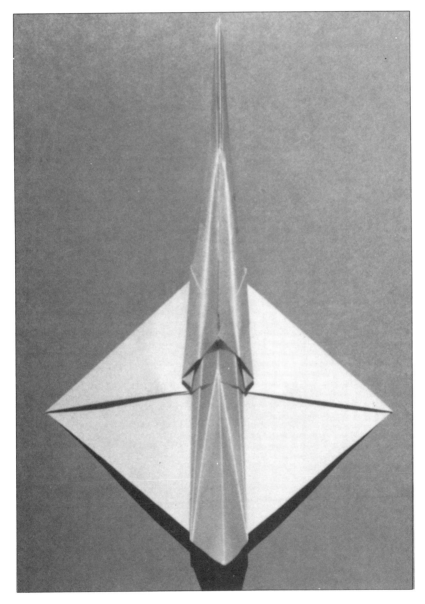

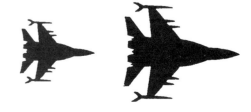

F-14 TOMCAT

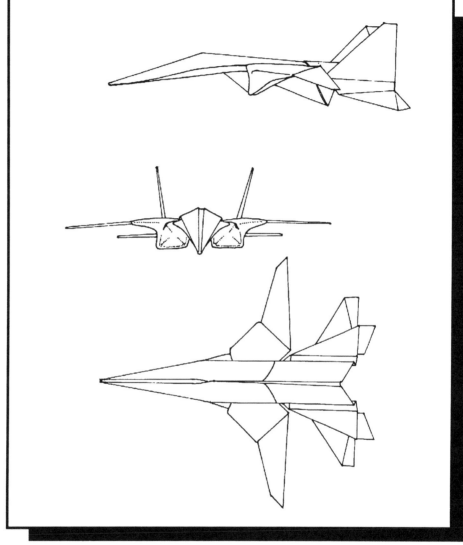

You won't be able to make this plane unless you have mastered the F-15 and other prior techniques. But by now you should be well disciplined in the art of folding. You're about to receive your "Top Gun U.S. F-14 Tomcat Trophy" for achieving the pinnacle in the art of paper airmanship. This plane will dazzle your eyes. Its structure is that of a real F-14 Tomcat and it will emulate the Tomcat's performance as well. This is the last, and the best of all the paper airplanes. You can fly it or treasure it, but make sure this plane is symmetrical & sturdy. For practice you may use an 8½ x 11 sheet of typing paper, but if you want the Tomcat to perform, use a 12½ x 15 or larger sheet of thin but strong paper. In making the Tomcat, turn back to the F-15 section & do Steps 1-7. Then turn back here. (If you find you are unable to start at the F-15, you'll need to go back to the Jet & begin there. Your first plane might not come out perfectly, but I'm sure you'll master it after a few tries.

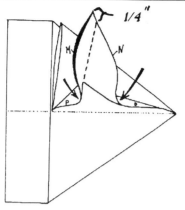

1/4"

F-15

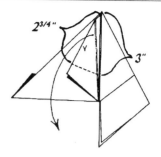

2 3/4" 3"

3) Fold Wing V down as shown here and align with the fuselage.

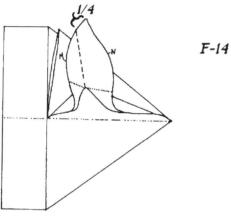

1/4

F-14

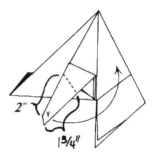

2"   1 3/4"

4) Your fold should look exactly like this. Now fold up toward the right. Remember to make crisp folds.

1) After you have completed Steps 1-7 of the F-15, your plane should look like this. Instead of having the dotted line on the N side of the wing like the F-15, make the dotted line on the M side as shown above. Don't let this change confuse you. Now, turn back to the F-15 section for steps 8-19, then return here.

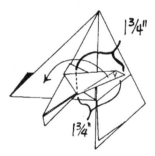

1 3/4"   1 3/4"

5) Your fold should look exactly like this. Now fold straight to the left.

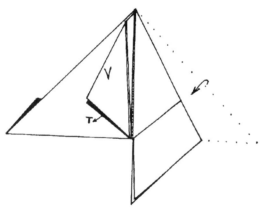

2) Fold Wing V to the left. Now your plane should look like this

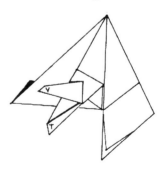

6) Your V wing should look like this. Make an even-opposite fold, following Steps 3-6, on the other side.

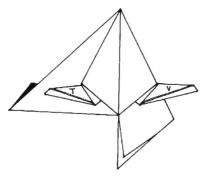

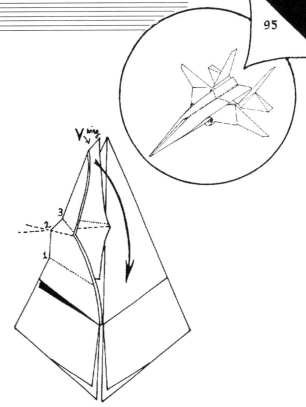

7) When the left side is finished, separate the sides and your plane should look like this. Look at the wings carefully now. You will be tucking the wings next but they will have this same definite appearance when finished. (The purpose of this tuck is to make the wings more rigid and sturdy.)

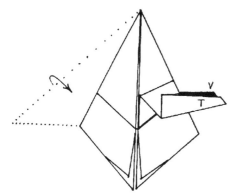

10) Very carefully open Wing V & fold down on Crease Line 2. (Simply tuck in the wing, downward, along dotted Crease Line 2.)

8) Flip the left Wing T over to the right and fold the left side to the middle. Your plane should look like this.

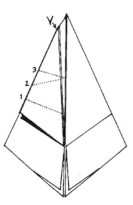

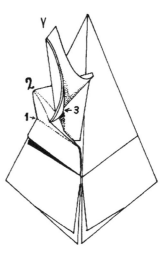

11) Fold it back up on Crease Line 3. Make sure Crease Line 3 is tucked in between Creases 1 & 2 exactly as shown here. Close the wing's side together so it looks like Step 7.

9) Unfold both wings, flip Wing V to the left and the plane should look like this. Crease Lines 1, 2 & 3 should be visible. (Note: you must know or mark the 3 crease lines.)

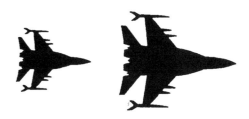

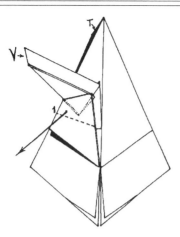

12) Your wing fold should look like this. Fold down on Crease Line 1.

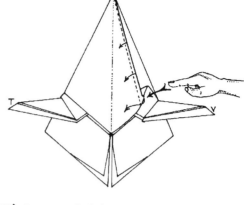

14B) As you fold, put your finger in the pocket where the arrow is pointing. Roll your finger toward the center of the fuselage. Flatten the small triangle.

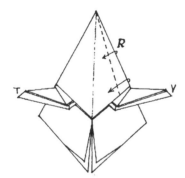

13) Your plane should look like this. Carefully repeat Steps 10-12 on left Wing T.

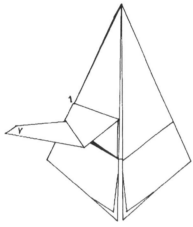

15) Your plane should look like this. Do the same on the left side.

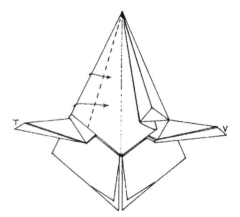

14A) Finish the left side and separate the wings; your plane should look like this. Fold Edge R halfway to the center along the dotted line.

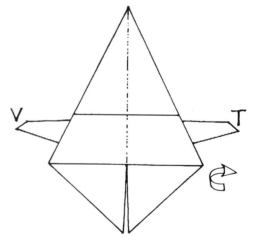

16) Turn the model over and your plane should look like this.

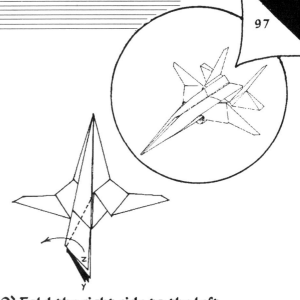

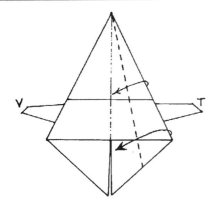

17) Fold the right side to the middle along the dotted line.

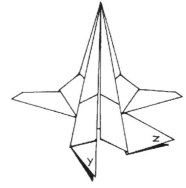

20) Fold the right side to the left. Flip Side Z over onto Side Y and fold to the left along the dotted line.

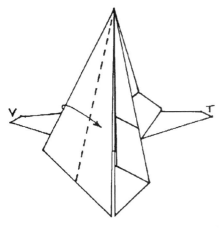

18) Your fold should look like this. Do the same on the left side.

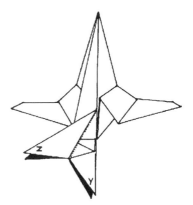

21) Fold fold-out to the left should look like this.

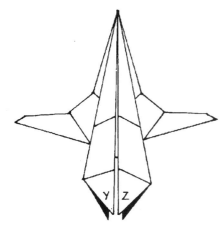

19) Your plane should look like this.

22) Flip Side Z back to the right. Do the same on the left side.

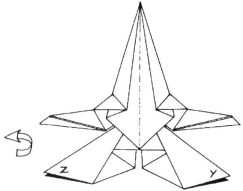

2) Turn the plane over and it should look like this.

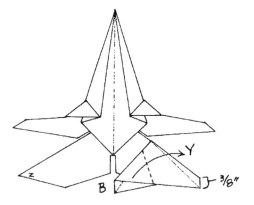

26) Your fold should now look exactly like this. Fold Stabilizer B toward Tail Fin Y on the dotted line.

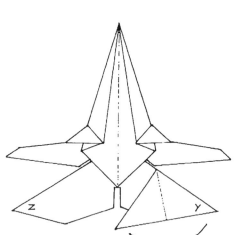

24) Unfold the right side stabilizer and the tail fin.

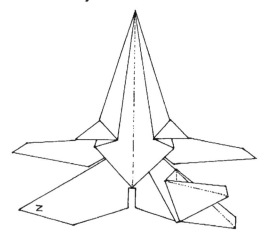

27) The fold to the right should look like this. Do the same on the left side.

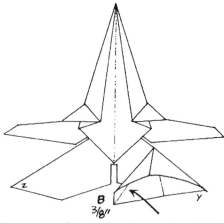

25) Put your finger in the pocket indicated by the arrow. Slowly move your finger upward, creating Edge B.

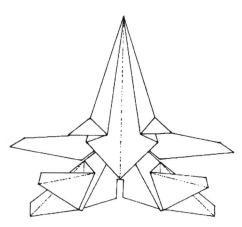

28) Your tail folds should look like this.

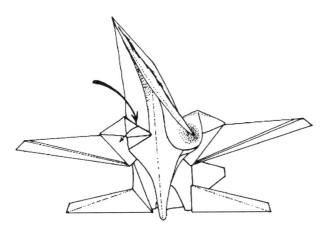

29) Now fold the nose down and align the back as you did on the F-15. Then fold the tail up. Next, put your finger in the pocket indicated by the big arrow and pull out for the engine.

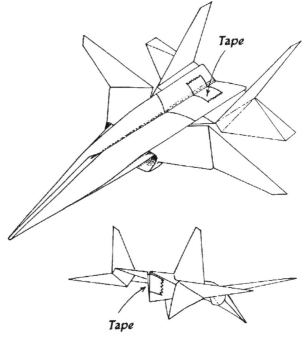

Tape

Tape

31) Put some tape in the spots shown here and your plane will be ready to fly. Throw the plane straight out from your body and it will fly smoothly.

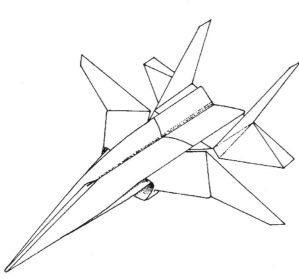

30) The finished version of the F-14 Tomcat!

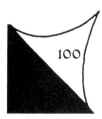

F-86 SABRE

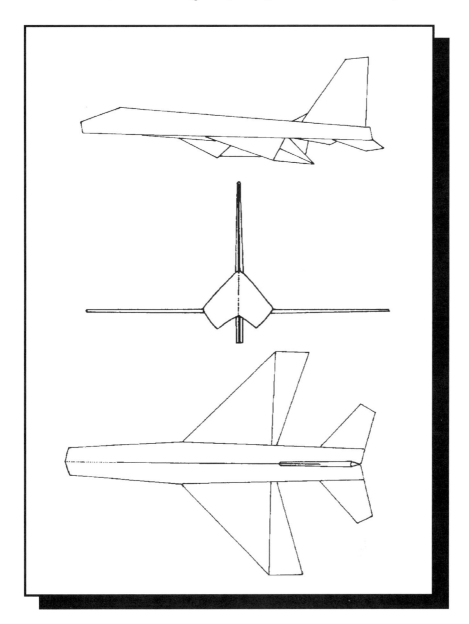

Thay Yang's F-86 Sabre model has never before been put into print. It uses more advanced folds than even the F-14, and it is recommended that you complete all the other models before folding this plane.

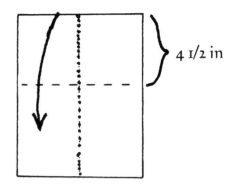

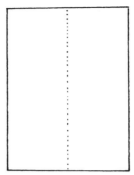

1) Book-fold paper in half, then unfold it.

2) Fold paper down.

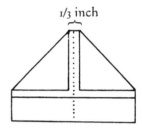

4 1/2 in

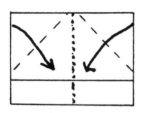

3) Fold corners down.

1/3 inch

4) The fold should look like this.

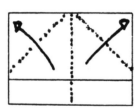

5) Unfold completely.

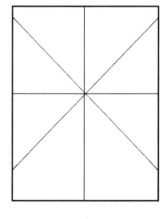

6) Turn the model over.

102

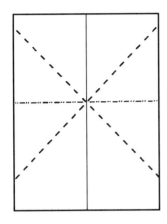

7) Press the center point with your finger, and the paper will fold upwards.

flat top toward you

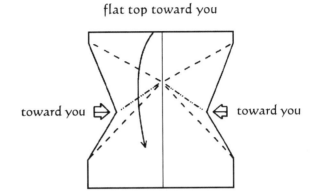

toward you ⇨　　　⇦ toward you

8) This is the folding diagram for the base. Fold the sides in and the top down.

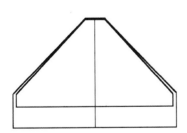

9) Base completed.

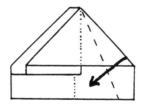

10) Fold towards center to look like next diagram.

11) Make a match-
ing fold for the
left side.

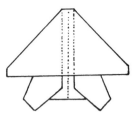

12) Flatten the plane
so it looks like this.

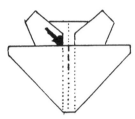

13) Cut or tear on
dashed line to look
like next step.

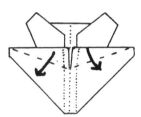

14) Fold edge
up.

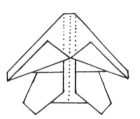

15) Reverse this fold
to the inside.

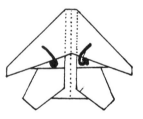

16) Completion of
fold to the in-
side.

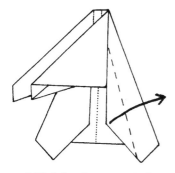

17) Fold edge to right side to look like next step.

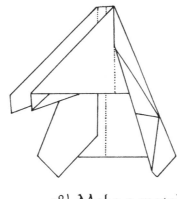

18) Make a matching fold for the left side.

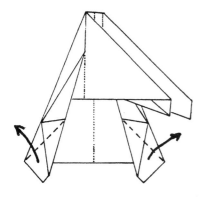

19) Fold stabilizers out to the sides.

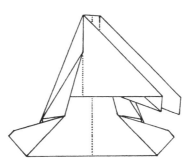

20) The stabilizers should look like this diagram.

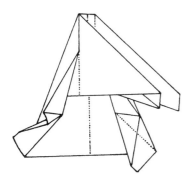

21) Unfold stabilizers back down and make an inside-reverse fold out again.

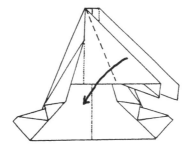

22) Completion of inside-reverse fold for the stabilizers. Book fold flap across center.

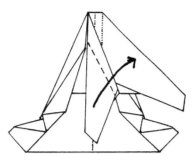

23) Fold flap up on dashed line.

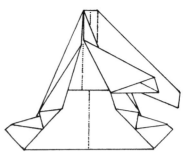

24) The wing folds out like this diagram. Make a matching fold for the right side.

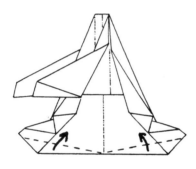

25) The edges fold up as shown on this diagram.

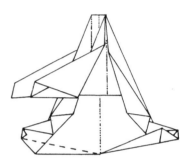

26) Both edges should look like the right side of this diagram.

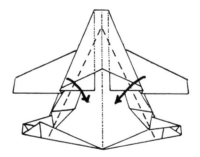

27) Insert right stabilizer under the flap that had been behind it. Do same to the left side. Make the fuselage fold.

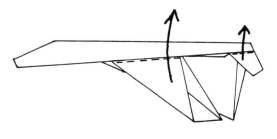

28) Completion of fuselage fold.
Fold wings and stabilizers up.

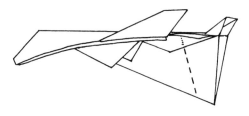

29) To create the tail, do an inside-reverse
fold: fold the belly of the plane up between
the wings to get a pointed tail, then fold
the top of the tail back down into itself to
give the tail its correct shape.

(See **Inside-Reverse Fold** in the front of
the book if you need help.)

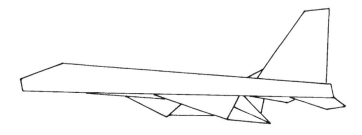

30) Completed F-86 Sabre!

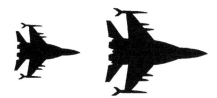

About the Author

Thay Yang is an award-winning illustrator, paper airplane designer, and model-rocket builder. He is the author of *Exquisite Interceptors* (Cypress House) and co-author (with John Collins and Dan Garwood) of *Return to the Fold* (Ten Speed Press). A senior aesthetics award winner in the *Great International Paper Airplane Contest* when he was only eighteen, Thay Yang has achieved worldwide recognition as a master folder.